DUTCH OVEN
COUNTRY STYLE

LOG CABIN GRUB IS REAL HAPPY TO BE ABLE TO SHARE ALL our FAVORITE DUTCH OVEN RECIPES WITH YOU ENTHUSIASTS. I HOPE YOU WILL TAKE TIME TO READ THE HELPFUL HINTS AND ALWAYS REMEMBER TO READ A RECIPE ALL THE WAY THROUGH JUST IN CASE YOU GET A SURPRISE. THERE ARE SOME GREAT DUTCH OVEN COOKS AROUND AND A LOT THAT YOU DON'T EVEN KNOW. ASK QUESTIONS OF THE PEOPLE AROUND YOU, SOMETIMES THEY KNOW MORE THAN YOU THINK. DUTCH OVENS HOLD A LOT OF MEMORIES FOR ME, ESPECIALLY THE ONE WHERE MY SON LARRY SHOWED HIS FELLOW SCOUTS HOW TO COOK A SNAKE. THE OVEN MAKES EVERYTHING TENDER

ENJOY- YOU'LL LEARN TO LOVE it. ALL RECIPES TRIED AND TASTED MANY TIMES.

AUTHOR -- COLLEEN SLOAN
ILLUSTRATED BY COUSIN SALTY: (SANDRA, "THE MAGIC FINGERS", VICARS).

Log Cabin Grub
900 Carnation Dr.
Sandy, Utah 84094

801-571-0789
888-596-1515
801-523-6240 FAX

"LET'S GO DUTCH."

Thanks for buying my Books — Colleen

1

STANDARD CAN MEASUREMENTS

Small 8 oz. can-------- 1 cup
#300 can-------------- 1 3/4 cup
1 tall---------------- 2 cups
303 can------------- 2 cups
2 can---------------- 2 1/2 cups
2 1/2 can----------- 3 1/2 cups
3 can---------------- 4 cups
5 can---------------- 7 1/4 cups
10 can-------------- 10 cups

These should help a little with measurements, you know how close I measure.

OVEN TEMPERATURES

Slow Oven------------ 250/300 degrees
Moderate Oven------- 325 degrees
Moderate------------- 350 degrees
Moderate Quick------ 375 degrees
Moderate Hot-------- 400 degrees
Hot------------------- 425-450 degrees
Extremely Hot------- 475-500 degrees

As you become more acquainted with your <u>Dutch Oven</u> you will discover how versatile it really is. The uses and variety of dishes you can cook will really temp you to cook more and experiment with new recipes. I love attending demonstrations where Dutch Oven cooking is going on. Your talent is waiting to be discovered. If all else fails, buy a dog. I'm only joking, my dog loves my cookin.

Dutch Oven's are a self timing oven as you will learn through out my books. As a challenge to you, try this, Put your favorite recipe in a warmed and lightly greased <u>Dutch oven</u> and place it on 350 degrees in your oven at home. Do not time it, just wait for the smell to tell you when it's done.

ITS DONE.

2

CONTENTS

Copyright July 2000
Eighth printing

3

SOME TOOLS TO MAKE IT EASIER

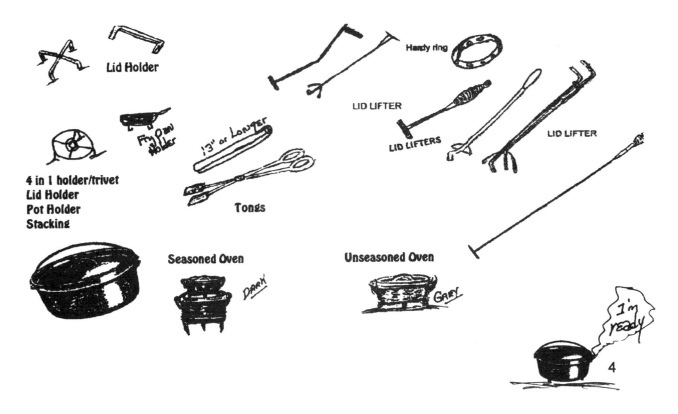

Lid Holder

Handy ring

LID LIFTER

LID LIFTERS

LID LIFTER

Fry Pan Holder

13" or Longer

4 in 1 holder/trivet
Lid Holder
Pot Holder
Stacking

Tongs

Seasoned Oven

DARK

Unseasoned Oven

GREY

I'm ready

4

COOKIN FOR FUN WITH DUTCH OVEN

I guess from the very beginning, I have been a Dutch Oven fan. I actually got started with my dad, because he was in Scouting for 38 years. Dutch Oven has been a standard for scout cooking because of its versatility. It just wouldn't seem right not to have Stew or Chili in a Dutch Oven for winter camp.

The Dutch oven, like the Indians, was pushed into a back corner by our advancing civilization. Whenever any one came upon one, Grandma knew what it was and basically how to use one. Though mostly forgotten, the DUTCH OVEN is rich in American History and Tradition. Whenever a Mountain man or Prospector was around, you would usually see one hanging from the packhorse. Trail drives and Chuck Wagons were always equipped with several. It made sense to cook with one, cause the lid kept the dust out and the heavy pot would not blow over.

Although they have changed in size, looks and even lost there legs, in some cases they are still as useful as ever and the briquettes have made them easier to use and more inventive in gourmet cooking. If you ever get the chance to attend a Cook-off sponsored by the International Dutch Oven Society, you'll taste some of the best food ever to cross your tongue. You can't help but go back for seconds.

REMEMBER THAT THE ONLY WAY TO DRY CAST IRON IS TO RETURN THE POT TO THE HEAT AND EVAPORATE THE MOISTURE.

COOKIN DUTCH {cont.}

If ever the Old West would come to your mind, just pull out the old black pot and hang it over the campfire on a tripod. Smell the smoke of a thousand campfires and picture the Pioneer women preparing a one pot supper after a long days walk. Hear the cowboys humming a tune as they wait for the camp cook to holler "Come and Get it.".

Lids off,---- the smell of Campfire Beans with Side Pork, and Sour Dough Dutch Oven Bread makes your mouth water.

The name DUTCH OVEN is used quite loosely. It actually applies to any cast iron pot with a lid on it. But, in all reality, the true basic Dutch Oven was a heavy cast iron skillet with straight sides and a fairly tight fitting lid. The bottom is flat, and it may or may not have legs. My first pot did not have legs, but I now ,most of them do.

Your DUTCH OVEN will serve you well if you take proper care of it and treat it with respect. The care of your DUTCH OVEN could make it's life time indefinite but we will cover that on another page.

Top   Bottom

Charcoal Placement

Always more heat on top than on bottom, when cooking with briquettes only

6

SEASONING YOUR DUTCH OVEN

Well, you just bought your first Dutch Oven and now your gonna take it home. As you are leaving the store, the salesperson tells you to be sure to season it before you use it. Oh boy, your thinking, what does that mean?

If you ask 100 people how to season a Dutch Oven, you'll probably get 15 different answers. Most Dutch Ovens today are coated with a protective substance by the manufacturer and all you need do is heat your oven & scrub it in warm soapy water, rinse it thoroughly with warm water, put it on the stove and heat it thoroughly to dry it. This is the only way to evaporate the moisture from the pot. Then, lightly grease it. Put it back in your regular oven or on your VOLCANO outdoor stove with 15 briquettes and bake it at 450 or 500 degrees for 1 hour. This bakes a protective grease coating into the pot and virtually give your pot a no-scrub surface. If the pot appears to be sticky, return to the oven or fire for 1/2 hr. longer. Be sure you lightly grease the oven. After 1 hour, you can give the oven another light coat of oil. I always turn my Dutch Ovens upside down so no grease will puddle in the bottom.

If your pot is seasoned well and used often, you will find it very easy to clean. If my pots are cleaned while they are hot, they can almost be wiped out with VINEGAR water and virtually no scraping. I mix my Vinegar 1 part V. to 4 parts Water and keep it in a spray bottle in my food box so I will have it every where I go. Vinegar is a great disinfectant and a natural Tenderizer for all foods. After most dishes, you should be able to wipe it out with a paper towel to clean it. Any oil or shortening will do, to season. I love the taste of Bacon, so I use a real light coat of bacon grease.

7

Care and Storing of your Oven

When storing your oven, be sure that you place a couple paper towels inside to make sure that any moisture that forms will be absorbed by the paper towel. If rust forms in your pot, simply scour it out with a SOS type pad and re-grease it before you season it again. As you cook with it you will re-season it each time. Seasoning the cast iron oven in your home oven can cause an odor in your home if you have not scrubbed off the protective coating. If you store your ovens after heating them to dry them out, with out oiling them, you will never have to worry about rancid oil. If you use to much oil and it becomes rancid it will be easily detected by the spoiled smell of the pot when opened. The grease actually goes rather yellow-orange, looks like a gummy texture. Simply fill your oven with wate, add a cup of apple cider Vinegar and boil; for a 1/2 hour on the stove. Pour out water. You should be able to scrape or scour out the rancid grease and then lightly re-grease or oil while it is hot, and turn it upside down in a hot (400 or better) oven on a cookie sheet or on your Volcano with 15 briquettes, to lightly re-season.

Be sure to heat your pot and lightly grease it before you use it again. If you have the storage bags they are nice to keep you ovens clean. But I do not suggest plastic because it will make your oven sweat and cause rust.

If your oven gets real rusty, sand blasting, soak in coke, scour with SOS for surface rust only, or soak in hay and I cup apple cider vinegar and enough water to cover your pan.. Just look in the yellow pages of your phone book under sand blasting. Everyone has their secrets and you need to practice with your oven and do what suits you best. The more you try the better it will get. Like Mama used to say, "Practice will make Perfection Happen".

YOUR DUTCH OVEN WILL BE YOUR BEST FRIEND IF YOU USE IT.

" Clean Em Hot. "

8

Judging the right temperature

There are a few important things to remember about a Dutch Oven. The 2/3rds rule is one of them and applies to every size.

BAKING: When using the Black Pot to bake in, the heat must be distributed on the top and bottom to maintain the proper temperature. Usually a 350 to 375 temp. is sufficient to bake most any dish. If you are in the wind it will take away some of your heat, but the following chart should help. You can raise or lower the temp by adding 1 briquette for every 18 to 20 degrees you wish to add to the cooking temperature.

Oven Size	8"	10"	12"	14"	16"	22"
Top Coals	11	13	15	17	19	25

Oven Size +3

In your Volcano, 12 Briquettes with no top heat will keep your oven at 350 to 375 using the damper.

Oven Size	8"	10"	12"	14"	16"	22"
Bottom Heat	6	8	10	12	14	20

Oven size minus 2

Arranging the briquettes so that the heat remains even is also very important. Place your coals in a circle underneath and on top. Never coals in the middle underneath. Baking can be a lot of fun in a Dutch Oven but proper heat and the 2/3rds rule are important factors. The smell will tell you when its done. But you can time it if you wish. Lifting the lid will add extra time to the cooking. Use a good name brand of briquettes for a more even heat. Briquettes are a great storage fuel, they don't evaporate or gel up.

JUDGING (CONT:)

FRYING: For frying, boiling or steaming of any dish, there should be only bottom heat. If you wish to simmer for awhile, remove more than 1/2 of the heat from the bottom. A Tripod is an excellent tool for this type of cooking, because it is so easy to raise or lower against the heat. Using briquettes to cook with, will help to save the trees and digging fire pits. With a DUTCH OVEN, it is very easy to practice NO TRACE CAMPING. It is much easier to regulate your heat with briquettes than over an open fire. As your briquettes burn down, there heat also declines. To maintain the proper temperature, add briquettes as necessary to keep the heat fairly constant. A charcoal starter is excellent to keep briquettes always ready and available. My grandmother used to judge her stove temperature by throwing a two finger pinch of flour on the stove top. If the flour did not brown in 5 minutes, the stove temperature was under 250 degrees. If it was brown in less than a minute, the oven was about 350 degrees and just right to bake bread. Most people have there own method of heat testing, but I have found the above chart to work well for me. Remembering the 2/3rds rule and the proper amount of briquettes has proven to work well on breads, rolls cakes, puddings and etc. I sincerely hope you will experiment with your oven and try many different dishes. Waiting for the smell to tell you when it is done is the easy way to cook. In a volcano, just put 12 briquettes in and cook. In a log cabin potbelly, use 12 briquettes and wait for the smell. Follow the temp. Guide on page 9 for briquettes and over an open campfire, be sure there are no coals underneath, only coals stacked on top and around the sides. Campfires are 1200 to 1600 degrees so cook with care. Always warm your oven slowly so you don't cause stress cracks from heating to fast.

There's a new Cast Iron Pot on the market by **Texport** it's a great oven!

10

CLEANING YOUR OVEN

On page 4 we briefly touched on the care of your oven. A lot of people will tell you never to wash the insides of your pot with soap, but I have found on occasion that I have had too. I have a pot of my Dads that is 55 years old and has been washed several times. It has no legs and today still cooks as good as any of my brand new ones. These pots are not fragile, but still require a certain amount of care. Dropping them or banging them against a hard surface could crack them and then their ability to hold the hot moisture that cooks your food is gone.

When you wash a pot use only a mild detergent and always rinse thoroughly. It is important to heat your pan and thoroughly dry it before storing it. I always clean my pans hot because it helps to release the food particles. I find it helpful to return the pot to the heat after emptying it, and spraying in a little vinegar water to soften the food. Then I wipe it clean with paper towels and store the pots in a dry place with a clean sheet of paper towel inside to keep the moisture from rusting my oven. You take care of them and they'll do you proud. The 1 part vinegar & 4 parts water is a great cleaning agent and disinfectant. The Apple Cider Vinegar is something I learned from my Pioneer Grandparents and mom.

It is not necessary to oil them before putting them away, but if you do be sure to wipe them out thoroughly with a paper towel to avoid rancid oil build up

Always use the right tools.

ONE of your Best Friends with A D.O.

PAPER TOWEL

"Clean em while they are Hot"

11

THINGS YOUR GONNA NEED

I thought I might try to give you an idea of the things you should have to make your cooking easier and allot more fun. You should always remember that briquettes are extremely hot so some ideas of handling them are as follows:

Matches
Gloves should go above the wrist
Long handled Tongs {the beat idea}
Long handled
Long handled Forks
Large and Small Knife
Can Opener
Cutting Board
Tool Kit
Briquettes

Hot Pads
Paper Towels (a must)
Vegetable peeler
Small Damp Towel or cloth
Measuring cups and spoons
Aluminum Foil
Lid Lifter
Spray Bottle for oil & vinegar water
Long Tongs
Wash Pan

Some of these things are not necessary every time, but needed more often than not. I hope you'll give DUTCH OVEN cooking your best shot and learn to enjoy this wonderful, healthy way of cooking.

IF YOU'R COOKING ON A VOLCANO, OR A LOG CABIN POT BELLY, YOU'LL USE LESS BRIQUETS AND COOK FASTER. NO MESS, FEWER BRIQUETS, LESS CHANCE TO GET BURNED, AND A CONTAINED FIRE, APPROVED BY THE RANGERS FOR NO OPEN FIRES.

I'm READY

the smell

12

NO MORE BURNED FINGERS

It has been my experience around Dutch Ovens, that sometimes people tend to get a little careless. For that reason, I wanted to give you a few safety tips. I've had my share of burns and treated a few Scouts that got burned. So-- I hope to save you the HURT. Spray your burns with the vinegar water to tenderize the skin and release the heat.

1. Before cooking with hot briquettes, always clean around the cooking area.

2. Always assume that any loose laying briquettes could be hot, and treat them accordingly.

3. Never attempt to move a hot oven without gloves, lid lifter, or hot pad.

4. Hot cooking oven build a lot of steam, always be careful which way you lift the lid.

5. When frying or deep frying, remember that hot grease burns are the worst kind.

6. Never let any clothing item, paper, plastic or flammable object come close to the briquettes.

Preventive medicine is the best cure for accidents. Stop them before they happen. Cooking with a Dutch Oven should be a pleasurable experience. The safety depends on you.
KNOW YOUR BRIQUETTES AND HOW THEY WORK BEFORE ATTEMPTING TO USE THEM IN AN ENCLOSED AREA.

OH MY GOSH!--HERE COMES COMPANY

Cooking for a lot of company is not a problem with a Dutch Oven. You see it is quite easy to do if you have an idea of how many to cook for. A 14 " Dutch Oven should easily hold 28 to 30 pieces of chicken and with 2 pieces each, you can feed 14 people with a 14" Dutch oven. This rule does not always apply, because cooking a roast for 14 people could very well not fit in a 14" unless it is a deep pot. Divide your pieces of meat as follows.

Chicken	1 person	2 pieces
Beef roast	1 person	¼ lb.
Turkey	1 person	1/3 lb.
Ribs	1 person	3 ribs

If you figure out what each person will eat, and multiply it by the amount of people you will feed, you will know your required amount of meat. A 12" shallow is the most popular size Dutch Oven but if you cook for more that 5 or 6, you will be wise to have a 12" deep also. If you want to learn to cook in a Dutch Oven, try doing it in your home oven first to get the feel. If you watch a demo somewhere, you'll be able to pick up a lot of pointers and see the different techniques of cooking. It's really fun and rewarding to turn out something great. The taste beats all. Seeing it done is half the battle of learning. Dutch Oven demo's are all around you and this almost lost art of cooking is something your gonna love to do. "Thanks for Droppin by."

14

"Wrap with tin Foil when windy"

STACKING DUTCH OVENS

Stacking the Dutch Ovens will depend on how many you intend to feed and if you are going to prepare more than a one dish meal. Stacking saves on briquettes, but the cooking times of each oven is also important. Your roast or spareribs may need 2 hours and bread only 45 minutes. Wind will have a tendency to make the briquettes burn hotter. Damp weather will make your briquettes burn slower and less heat. Keep the briquettes off the wet ground. A simple fire blanket or foil will accomplish this. Simple tin foil wrapped around 3 sticks in the ground can help to divert the wind. Be sure to replenish your heat source when needed. The average size briquette lasts at full heat value for 25 to 30 minutes. On the previous page I have given you a simple formula for unexpected company. I hope you can enjoy the recipes that follow and will try some of your own. If you should invent a new recipe I'd love to hear from you. Sharing Dutch Oven fun is what makes the Oven cookin appear to be so friendly.

Stacking can be alot of fun. It takes some practice but its impressive + amazing to watch em cook.

TRIPODS AND THEIR USES

I guess the reason that I like the tripod so much, is that it is so easy to pack around. It keeps the oven off the ground and helps to regulate the heat. Raising and lowering the oven is easy and it is safer because you are farther from the heat. A few drawing are here to show you the versatility of the tripod. Now remember I'm not the artist, I do the cookin. My cuzin salty has the magic fingers. I sure do appreciate her help and if you need her, she's available. Not free but reasonable.

Old black pot cookin was done mostly over open fires with a tri-pod or fire irons. What a great way to show your talents. It's impressive to see the moisture escape and get that wonderful aroma of Dutch Oven cookin'.

"Its a way to cook like the Pioneers."

16

ONE-POT RECIPE FIXIN'S FOR DUTCH OVEN

SECTION ONE:

When it's time to go campin, nothing is worst than trying to pack enough stuff to make those gourmet meals and get fancy. It's real easy to throw in one or two stackable Dutch ovens, a tripod, briquettes and a starter bucket with your camp box. So, I'm gonna try to give you a lot of one dish meals to start off with and then maybe get a little fancy later. When the mountain men, pioneers and early settlers tried to cook they didn't have time to get fancy but it had to be good food. When your out with a bunch of scouts it's a lot easier to clean up after one-dish meals. So, enjoy these recipes and try them at your leisure. You'll be amazed at the difference in flavor with the Dutch Oven compared to your oven. And remember anything cooked in your oven can be cooked in a Dutch Oven and visa-versa. Experiment now and then with spices and see what kind of flavors you can come up with. Let me suggest some of the following spices to keep around for Dutch Oven cooking.

Salt & Pepper (of Course), Dried & fresh Onions, Red Pepper, Chili Powder, Cumin, Definitely Garlic, Dry Mustard, Worcestershire Sauce, Celery Salt & Fresh Celery, Teriyaki Sauce, Vinegar, Dried Green Peppers, Liquid Smoke, Soy Sauce, Corn Starch, Brown Sugar, Ginger, Paprika & Molasses. Other food products such as, Cream soups, Mushroom-Celery-Chicken-, Green Chili's, Can Mushrooms, Bar-B-Que. Sauce, Pork & Beans, Kidney Beans, Catsup, Chili Sauce, Beef Broth, Cooking Oil, Tomato Sauce, and anything that fits your recipes.

THE ORIGINAL DUTCH OVENS WERE MADE OF CAST IRON, BUT TODAY ANYTHING THAT RESEMBLES IT WITH A LID IS CALLED A DUTCH OVEN.

17

CHICKEN & POTATO CASSEROLE

1 Bag hash brown potatoes (Thawed)
1 1/2 tsp. Salt
2 Cups cut up chicken (cooked)
1 Cup shredded cheddar cheese
2 Tbsp. onion
16oz. Sour Cream
1 Can Condensed Cream of Chicken Soup
1 Can Condensed Cream of Celery Soup
1 Pkg. frozen Chopped Broccoli (thaw & Drain)
Mix potatoes and the remaining ingredients
Together in Dutch oven, bake for 25 min. Lift lid and
spread with cheese (this is a good time to add biscuits
if wanted. Bake another 15min or wait for the smell.
Remove from fire and your ready to eat.

WRANGLER PIE

10 potatoes cooked and mashed
2 c. string beans
2 c. cream mushroom soup
2 lbs. ground beef
1 med. onion diced
1 c. grated cheese
Cook ground beef with onion, drain off fat
add beans and soup. Spread mashed potatoes on top,
can be instant. Sprinkle cheese over potatoes & cook
for 10 more minutes until cheese is melted. This can be
done in a 12" Dutch oven.

Um-Um
Good

18

JOSE'S LASAGNA

This is a Real Good ONE.

1 1/2 lb., hamburger
1 large chopped onion
1 tsp. salt---1 tsp. pepper
1 1/2 tsp. cumin---1/4 tsp. red pepper
1 tbs. chili powder
2 c. stewed tomatoes
2 Cups Cottage Cheese
1 Cup Grated White Cheese

Combine all ingredients and cook until meat is well done. Line the bottom of a 12" Dutch oven with tortilla shells. Spoon 1/2 of the mixture over shells, then spread 1-Cup Cottage Cheese and 1/2 Cup Grated white cheese. More tortilla shells, 1c. cottage & 1/2 grated white cheese. Bake for 30 minutes at about 350/375 degrees. Serve topped with chopped olives, onions, and green peppers & grated white cheese.

HOT-DOG DELUXE

You can serve it in a Bun or a Tortilla shell.

1 c. chopped onions
1 c. chopped celery
1 c. catsup
1 lemon & 1/4 c. brown sugar
1/4 c. Worcestershire sauce
2 tbs. vinegar & 1 tbs. mustard
1/2 c. water & 12 hot-dogs

In 12" Dutch Oven, put 2 tbs. cooking oil. Slice hot dogs & add to pot with onions and celery. Simmer 3 to 5 min. Squeeze lemon and add juice along with all other ingredients and simmer until the sauce is thick & clings to the meat. Serve in buns, on tortilla shells on crackers, in bread bowls on rice or what ever. A 12" oven will require about 8 coals bottom and 8 top to simmer. Or, hang from tri-- pod, above the fire. This is an easy dish for camping and tastes good too.

19

DUTCH GREEN PEPPER STEAK

"Pork or Beef"

3 c. stew meat or cut up steak
¼ c. soy sauce -- ½ tsp. garlic
½ tsp. Ginger -- ¼ c. cooking oil
1 c. sliced green peppers
1 c. sliced onion
1 c. chopped celery
1 c. water
2 heaping tbsp. cornstarch
2 tomatoes cut in wedges

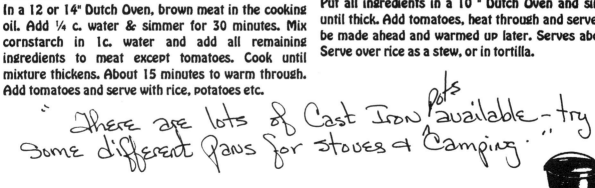

In a 12 or 14" Dutch Oven, brown meat in the cooking oil. Add ¼ c. water & simmer for 30 minutes. Mix cornstarch in 1c. water and add all remaining ingredients to meat except tomatoes. Cook until mixture thickens. About 15 minutes to warm through. Add tomatoes and serve with rice, potatoes etc.

SERGIO'S CHILI VERDE

"Cook'N sure is FUN"

4 c. cubed leftover roast beef, pork, or chicken
1 can stewed tomatoes
1 can green chilies
2 c. leftover boiled potatoes
1 med. can tomato sauce
1 tsp. salt – ½ tsp. pepper
½ tsp. chili powder— ¼ tsp. red pepper
¼ c. flour dissolved in 3 c. water

Put all ingredients in a 10" Dutch Oven and simmer until thick. Add tomatoes, heat through and serve. Can be made ahead and warmed up later. Serves about 6. Serve over rice as a stew, or in tortilla.

"There are lots of Cast Iron Pots available - try Some different Pans for stoues & Camping."

20

WESTERN SAUCE FOR ALL MEATS

1 c. catsup -- ¼ c. vinegar
2 tbsp. Worcestershire sauce
½ tsp. liquid smoke --- ¼ tsp. garlic
1 medium chopped onion
½ c. chopped celery
1 c. stewed tomatoes
¼ c. green peppers (optional)

The taste is Really good!

Place all ingredients in a 12" Dutch Oven greased, & simmer until all vegetables are well done. Bacon grease will add to the flavor. When sauce is done, you can add Pork Spareribs, Beef stew meat, any wild game, ribs, Lamb, Veal or Fish. If you wish, you can spoon the sauce over already cooked meat to enhance its flavor. This sauce can also be used as gravy over rice, potatoes or dressing.

QUICK TRAIL CASSEROLE

1 ½ lb. hamburger - 2 c. frozen peas
1 medium onion chopped - 1 tsp. salt
2 c. sliced celery - ¼ tsp. pepper
1 can mushroom soup - ¼ tsp. garlic
3 tbsp. milk - 1 pkg. Chinese noodles

"Good fast meal."

In a greased 12" Dutch Oven, cook the hamburger until done. Combine all other ingredients in the pot and cook at 350 degrees, for 20 minutes. Serve with soy sauce and dinner rolls. Makes a great one dish meal.

movin fast for Good food.

21

DUTCH OVEN TERIYAKI CHICK

14-16 pieces of chicken
1 c. brown sugar
1 bottle teriyaki sauce
(12 oz. or more)
1 onion sliced optional
1 tbsp. cooking oil)

Good Stuff

Put oil in Dutch Oven and arrange the chicken. This should require a 12"oven. Sprinkle brown sugar over the chicken and pour on the teriyaki. sauce. Cover and cook for 1 hour. Chicken will be pulling from the bone, Vegetables can be placed on top at about 45 minutes. 10 to 12 briquettes in your volcano. 10 on bottom 15 on top briquettes only. In your oven 350 degrees and wait for the smell.

DUTCH OVEN POT ROAST

1 large pot roast (3 to 5 lbs.   1 tsp. salt
1 medium onion sliced   ½ tsp. pepper
8 to 10 potatoes peeled   1 c. water
10/12 carrots peeled & cut in half
1 can cream of mushroom soup
2 tbsp. cooking oil (bacon grease)

Put cooking oil in bottom of Dutch Oven place the roast inside. Place onions on top Add remaining ingredients. and cover. About 90 minutes. Be sure to maintain the temperature. This one dish meal is excellent for outdoors. Briquettes can be added 15 minutes before serving.

12 Briquettes in your Volcano or Log Cabin Stove, wait for the smell.

A TBSP. OF APPLE CIDER VINEGAR ADDED TO THE WATER POACH EGGS WILL HELP TO SET THE WHITES SO THAT THEY WON'T SPREAD.

WHEN YOU BOIL EGGS, PUT SALT IN THE WATER AND THE SHELLS WON'T CRACK AS EASY.

It's the smell

22

DOOR SLAMMER CHICKEN

8 chicken breasts skinned & brown in DUTCH OVEN
Mix Together, 2-8 oz. Bottles of Russian Dressing.
1-12 oz. Bottle Apricot jam
1 pkg. Instant onion soup mix
Pour over chicken, and bake in oven for about 1½ hrs.
Heat should be 350 degrees, which in a 12" oven is 10
or 12 on bottom and 15 to 16 briquettes on top.
Replenish your briquettes as needed to maintain the
350 temperature. 12 Briquettes
in Volcano or Log Cabin Stove.

**YOUR OVEN WILL TELL YOU WHEN
IT'S DONE BY THE SMELL.**

ON THE TRAIL STEW

In a 12" Dutch Oven make a Lg. 1 lb. Hamburger Patty
to cover bottom of the pot.
Place 4 sliced carrots & 6 med. Sliced potatoes. Slice
one large onion over the top of the potatoes &carrots.
Sprinkle with salt and pepper or 1tsp. Log Cabin
Seasoning.
Cook for 25 minutes at 350 degrees. Can be served
with Dutch Oven bread. This is a meal that can also be
served as a tin foil dinner. Just wrap everything in foil
and cook on the open fire or BBQ grill.

**ONLY WAY TO DRY CAST IRON IS TO
HEAT IT UP AND EVAPORATE THE
MOISTURE.**

" These are real Crowd Pleasers "

23

SLOPPY JOES DONE COUNTRY

2 lbs. hamburger or left over roast
2 tbsp. oil or bacon grease
1 medium chopped onion
½ c. catsup   1 tsp. salt
½ tsp. sage   ½ tsp. pepper
2 tbsp. mustard   ½ cup brown sugar
1 tbsp. Worcestershire sauce
1 can cream chicken, mushroom or celery soup
(optional).

Worth a TRY"

Put oil in a 12"DUTCH OVEN and cook the hamburger. Add onion and other ingredients to hamburger. Cover and simmer on low heat (325) for 25 min be sure to keep heat low and not burn the bottom. 10 bottom 10 top briquettes only. 12 briquettes in volcano.

COUNTRY STYLE RIBS AND KRAUT

3 lbs. or 12 spareribs
2 tbsp. oil or bacon grease
2 large onions sliced
¼ tsp. salt
1/8 tsp. pepper
½ c. hot water
2 lbs. or 3 large cans Sauerkraut

EVEN I LIKE THIS ONE

Place ribs in a 12 " DUTCH OVEN. Add Salt, pepper, onion, garlic and water. Simmer Low heat (325) for 1/2 hour. Remove from heat and add sauerkraut. Cover & simmer 15 or 20 minutes until warm through. 5 or 6 people. Great dish for something different.
12 briquettes Volcano – 10 bottom 15 top for briquettes only.

24

MEAT AND POTATO PIE

1 pound hamburger
1 medium onion chopped (1/2 cup)
Chopped green pepper
Seasoning
2/3 cup water
1 small can stewed tomatoes
1 tsp. Real salt
½ tsp. Basil
3 cups stiffly mashed potatoes
½ cup grated cheese (white or cheddar)

In a 12" Dutch oven or skillet, brown onion, hamburger, green pepper and seasoning. Add water and tomatoes. Spread 2/3 of the mashed potatoes that you cooked earlier or have as leftovers, into a 12" Dutch oven. Spread the beef mixture into the bottom and cover with remaining potatoes. Sprinkle cheese on top and Bake for 25 min. at 350 degrees.

WESTERN CREOLE CHICKEN

The South goes west

8 chicken Breasts	1 tsp. Garlic powder
6 slices bacon	1 cup diced ham
1 cup chopped onions	2 cup stewed tomatoes
1 tbsp. Dry parsley	1 salt
½ tsp. Thyme	1/8 tsp. Tabasco sauce
2 cups boiling water	½ cup chopped celery

Wash chicken, remove skin, and spray with apple cider vinegar and sprinkle with garlic powder. Set aside. Place bacon in Dutch oven and cook until crisp. Remove bacon and crumble. Put chicken in oven and brown. Set chicken aside and put ham and onions in oven, brown and add bacon, chicken, tomatoes, parsley, Tobasco sauce, thyme, salt and water. Cover and cook for 35 minutes at 350. When done, thicken gravy by dissolving 2 tbsp. Of cornstarch in ¼ cup water and adding to chicken mixture. Great over rice or mashed potatoes.

12 briquettes in Volcano – 10 bottom 15 top briquettes only

" Can't get any easier than that "

25

BUNKHOUSE PORK CHOPS IN RANCH SAUCE

8 pork chops
1 c. water
2 tbsp. brown sugar
1 tsp. garlic powder
1/4 c. flour – ½ cup water
3 tbsp. catsup
1/4 c. chopped onion
1/2 c. sour cream
1 tbsp. seasoning

Place chops and following ingredients in a 12" Dutch Oven. Add 1 c. water, brown sugar, onion, garlic and season salt. Simmer for One hour and 30 minutes. Add flour to ½ cup water and add the sour cream and catsup. Pour over chops and return to heat. Heat thoroughly without boiling. Chops will be very tender.
Be careful with campfire not to use too much heat. No heat directly underneath.
12 briquettes in Volcano – 10 bottom 15 top briquettes Only
350 degree in your Volcano close damper ½ way and briquettes will last 2 hours

" Touch up your Pork chop taste with a sprinkle of sage + Thyme "

26

CAMPFIRE FRY BREAD AND CHILI

3 c. flour
4 tsp. baking powder
3 tsp. salt
2 tbsp. sugar
1 1/4 c. lukewarm water

Nothing says Lovin Like chili

Mix all ingredients together except liquid. Pour in water all at once. Mix to biscuit stage. The less you handle dough the better. Let stand for 5 minutes. Divide in 4 sections. Roll out 1/8 in. thick, cut into pieces and. fry in hot fat until golden brown. While chili is cooking, fry the bread and drain on paper towels. Cut up lettuce, tomatoes, grate cheese, chop onions, chop olives and bring sour cream to room temperature. When chili is ready, spoon over fry bread, sprinkle cheese and all other ingredients. Top with sour cream and serve. Makes a great meal. Fry in a 10" Dutch Oven or Wok.
BE SURE TO KEEP BRIQUETTES IN A CIRCLE AROUND THE OUTSIDE WALLS OF THE DUTCH OVEN, EXCEPT TO FRY OR SAUTE.

DUTCH OVEN CHILI

1 c. red or pinto beans.
1/4 tsp. pepper
1 tbsp. chili powder
1/2 tsp. seasoned pepper
1 can stewed tomatoes
1 lb. hamburger fried
1/2 c. grated carrots

1/2 c. apple cider vinegar
1 tsp. salt
1/2 tsp. garlic salt
1 med. onion chopped
1/4 c. catsup
2 tbsp. oil
1/4 tsp. cumin

In a 12 " Dutch put oil and add hamburger, salt onion and pepper. Brown and add all remaining ingredients. Simmer for 1 ½ hours over 10 briquettes in your volcano – 10 bottom 12 top with briquettes only and 350 degrees in you oven. If you did not soak beans it may take 2 hours or more to soften beans. Do not lift your lid.

27

CHUCKWAGON PORK CHOPS

6 pork chops
1 can cream of celery soup
1/4 tsp. thyme
1 c. carrots sliced
1/3 c. water

Brown pork chops in 12" Dutch Oven with a little oil. Add remaining ingredients and cover. Simmer for 45 to 50 minutes over 325 heat. Pork chops will be tender & gravy will form. Can be served with mashed potatoes or rice or eaten with biscuits and gravy. 12 briquettes in volcano – 15 top and 10 bottom briquettes only. 350 in your oven.

CHICKEN BEEF BREASTS

8 chicken breasts.............1 onion sliced
1 jar dried beef slices   8 slices bacon
1/2 tsp. salt   1/4 tsp. pepper
1 can cream mushroom soup
1 c. sour cream

It's different & Good.

Roll 1 slice bacon around each chick breast. place dried beef slice and onion in bottom of 12" Dutch Lay chicken on top of beef. Salt and pepper, Pour soup, sour cream & 1/2 cup water over the chicken, cover and bake At 350 degrees for 50 minutes or until meat pulls from the bones. 12 briquettes in volcano – 15 top and 10 bottom briquettes only 350 in your oven.

WHEN A RECIPE CALLS FOR CHICKEN BREASTS, YOU CAN SUBSTITUTE ANY PIECE OF CHICKEN.

"Don't forget to heat Em to dry Em"

28

CHICKEN PUFFS

6 breasts of chicken or 1 large can chicken meat.
1 8 oz pkg. cream cheese
1 tsp. salt
1/2 tsp. pepper
1/4 c. butter or margarine
2 tbsp. Worcestershire sauce
1/2 c. chopped black olives
1/2 c. chopped mushrooms
1/2 c. green chilies
1 small btle pimentos
1 can crescent rolls (12)

Boil the chicken and bone it out. Melt the butter in a fry pan and sauté the onions & mushrooms. Cut the chicken into small cubes, and mix with cream cheese & onion mixture. Add all other ingredients mix and roll into balls. Separate the crescent rolls and wrap around the balls of chicken. Place the rolls in a warm greased Dutch Oven and bake as directed on the package. Use the water from boiling the chicken as the broth for your gravy. Serve with rice and cover with gravy. You'll be surprised at the great taste. 12" Dutch Oven should be enough for this recipe. One can of cream of chicken soup, diluted with broth and poured over top can be your gravy

Dutch Oven cooks go from 0 to 350 in 6 to 10 minutes

29

COUNTRY POT ROAST

3 to 4 lb. roast (allow 1/2 lb. per person)
(Beef, pork, lamb, venison, elk etc.)
1/3 c. oil or bacon grease
2 tsp. salt   1/2 tsp. pepper
1 tsp. onion salt   1/2 tsp. celery salt
1 sprinkle garlic salt
1 medium onion sliced
1 c. water or beef broth

" Go for this one Guys" It's mouth watering"

Select Dutch Oven size according to the size of the roast. 3 to 4 lb. roast will feed 6 to 8 people. Warm the oven and melt the oil. Brown the roast on all sides. Add the spices and onion, pour in the water or broth. Cover and Cook over a low heat (325-350) for 1 hour. You can put in 1 carrot, 1 potato per person you plan to feed. Slowly simmer for another ½ hour or until you can smell it or see it vent. Spread mushrooms over the top if desired. When potatoes and carrots are cooked, remove from oven and keep warm. Dissolve 2-tbsp. corn starch in a small amount of water and add to broth. This will thicken and makes excellent gravy.

YOU MAY THINK IT SOUNDS SILLY TO COOK IN YOUR OVEN WITH A DUTCH OVEN, BUT IT WILL GIVE YOU LOTS OF PRACTICE AND THE TASTE IS GREAT. TRY IT. SET YOUR OVEN AT 350, WAIT FOR THE SMELL YOU BECOME FUEL EFFECIANT BECAUSE YOUR CAST IRON ABSORBS AND HOLDS IT'S HEAT.

The smell

30

COUNTRY DUTCH OVEN CHICKEN

16 pieces chicken
1 can cream celery
1 can cream mushroom
1 can cream chicken
1 bottle bar-b-Que. sauce
6 strips bacon

In a 12" Dutch Oven place the bacon strips and fry.
Place all other ingredients on top of bacon strips &
Sprinkle the top with salt and pepper. Cover and place
on the heat at 350 degrees. Cook for 45 minutes and
get ready for the treat of your life. This is a great
recipe for chicken. 12 briquettes in volcano – 15 top
and 10 bottom briquettes only 350 in your oven.

" You can win a Contest with
this ONE. "

LAYERED DUTCH BURGERS

In a 12 " Dutch Oven, cover the bottom with strips of
bacon. Warm the oven and place hamburger patties on
top of the bacon. Now place layers of potatoes and
carrots on top of meat. Salt and pepper pour 1 cup of
tomato juice over the top of mixture. Cook on 325 for
about 1 hour. Be sure meat is thoroughly cooked.
Tomato juice is optional.

VARIATIONS:
1/2 c. Beef Broth
1/2 c. teriyaki sauce
1 c. chopped celery
Substitute stew meat for hamburger
BBQ Sauce or stewed tomatoes for juice

FOR A COMPLIMENTARY FLAVOR TASTE, ADD A PINCH OF BASIL
OR CURRY TO HAMBURGER PATTIES. The only way to dry cast iron is to return it to the heat.

um-
um-

E Z BEEF STEW

2 lb. stew meat or hamburger
2 lg. onions chopped
10 medium potatoes
8 carrots   2 c. chopped celery
1 tsp. salt   1/2 tsp. pepper
1/2 tsp. garlic   1/2 tsp. thyme
2 tbsp. Worcestershire sauce

These are easy recipes but what a Reward. "

Place oil in Dutch Oven and brown the meat. Add chopped onion and sauté a few minutes longer. Add all other ingredients and 4 cups water. Simmer until all ingredients are tender. About 45 minutes at 350 degrees. Serve with your best Dutch Oven biscuits or corn bread. 14" Oven serves 12 to 14 Deep 12" will work well too. In your Volcano 12 briquettes, in a circle – 10 bottom 15 top for deep 12" 12 bottom 17 top for 14"

– Good – Good .. Great

RATTLE SNAKE BEANS

1-1/2 lb. smoked sausage
1 lb. bacon
2 medium chopped o
1/2 c. brown sugar
1/2 c. molasses
1/2 c crushed pineapple
6 c. pork and beans

THISSSSS IS A GOOD ONE

Cut bacon into small pieces and brown in DO. Put in onion and sauté till clear. Slice sausage and add to oven. stir in remaining ingredients and cover. Bake at 325 in a 12" DO for 30 minutes. 10 briquettes in volcano – 9 or 10 bottom 10 top with briquettes only.

If you can't get snake – try sausage.

COUNTRY PEPPER STEAK

1 round steak   1 onion sliced
1 sliced green pepper
3 slices bacon   1 tsp. Real salt
½ tsp. pepper
3-8 oz cans tomato sauce
½ tsp. garlic

The taste will tell.

In a 12" Dutch Oven, fry the bacon cut into pieces. Put steak in on top of bacon, or cut into small pieces if you prefer. Sprinkle with seasonings and add onion green pepper and tom sauce. Simmer for 1 ½ to 2 hours. Can be served over rice or with your favorite potato. * Simmer means cook gently in a liquid just below the boiling point. Feeds 4 people, double for more. In a 12": 10 on the bottom and 15 on the top. In your Volcano 12 briquettes and wait for the smell

PORCUPINE TRAIL BALLS

12 " Dutch Oven   Feeds 4 people
½ lb. Sausage
1 lb. ground beef
1 c. cooked rice
¼ c. chopped onion
½ tsp. salt   ¼ tsp. pepper
1-8 oz. can tomato sauce or BBQ sauce

~ A Good Company Dish.

Mix all ingredients together and shape into ball oblong shape. Place in greased DO and pour tomato sauce over top. Cook for 40 minutes over med. heat (350). Serve with your favorite potato or vegetable dish. (add 4 eggs and 1 cup cracker crumbs to stretch recipe) 12 briquettes on Volcano – shallow or deep Dutch Oven 10 Bottom 15 top briquettes only.

BREAD CRUMBS ADDED TO SCRAMBLED EGGS WILL IMPROVE THE FLAVOR AND ADD MORE HELPINGS. TRY FLAVORED ONES.

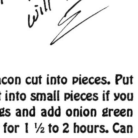

CHILI SAUCE BEANS

1/2 lb. bacon   1 lb. hamburger
1 lg. onion   1 green pepper
1/2 c. brown sugar
1/2 c. catsup
2 c. chili sauce
2 tbsp. mustard
2 c. cooked ham or lil smokies or sausage
2 extra lg. cans pork and beans or 1 gal.

Brown bacon and hamburger in 12" Dutch Oven that has been greased and warmed. Chop onion and pepper and sauté. Add remaining ingredients and simmer for 1 1/2 hours at about 275 or 300 degree. Stir the beans 2 or 3 times to prevent burning. 9 briquettes in Volcano – 8 bottom 10 top for briquettes only.

" Very Good "

DUTCH OVEN BAKED BEANS

1/2 lb. bacon, fry and remove grease
1 lb. hamburger
1 onion chopped
4 c. kidney beans(soak beans overnight in water)
1 c. lima beans   4 cans white beans
1 c. brown sugar   1/4 tsp. soda
1/3 cup apple cider vinegar
1 tbsp. liquid smoke
1 c. catsup

In a 12" Dutch oven, fry bacon and remove grease Add hamburger and fry, drain off grease and add all other ingredients to oven. Stir, cover and bake for 1 1/2 hours, on low heat. If beans have not been soaked, increase cooking time to 4 hours or till tender. 350 degrees in your oven. 12 briquettes in Volcano.

" This is Great "

TO KEEP YOLKS FROM CRUMBLING WHEN SLICING A BOILED EGG,
RUN YOU KNIFE UNDER WATER BEFORE EACH CUT.
SET EGGS IN A BOWL OF WARM WATER BEFORE USING
AS THIS RELEASES THE WHITES FROM THE SHELLS.

CHICKEN WINGS ALA COKE

When I ask my Scoutmasters if they had a favorite recipe, this is the one that Vic Tyler out of Troop 45 gave me. He said it was the easiest one he had ever cooked and the boys loved it. Put enough chicken wings in a 12" Dutch Oven to feed the boy 4 or 5 each. Add a big bottle of catsup and 1 3/4 cans of coke. Cover and cook at 350 degrees for 35 minutes. Drink the rest of the can of coke, and wait for the chicken to cook. Meat will pull from bones when done. Very simple and easy but tastes great. Takes about 40 minutes. Add a little salsa and curry or cayenne to spice it up.
12 briquettes in Volcano – 10 bottom 15 top briquettes only.

QUICK AS A TURKEY CASSEROLE

Thaw out a role of frozen ground turkey and roll it out flat. Make up a pkg. of Stove Top stuffing with the box directions and spread over turkey. Roll up into a ball or loaf and cook in a greased 12" Dutch Oven until lightly browned. Approximately 30 minutes at 350 degrees baking temperature. You can make gravy to pour over top if desired and simmer for an 10 minutes to warm through. Fast to fix and great taste. 1 can cream of chicken diluted with 1/2 c milk makes great gravy. Left over sliced turkey works well too.

(*You can wrap sliced Turkey around Dressing also!*)

IF YOU WANT TO MAKE A PECAN PIE AND HAVEN'T ANY NUTS, SUBSTITUTE CRUSHED CORN FLAKES.

" *This one's a scout favorite* "

35

ROASTING A TURKEY DUTCH OVEN STYLE

Thaw your turkey out completely before you try to cook it in a DUTCH OVEN. This makes the meat more pliable and easy to work with. Make sure that the turkey fits easily in the oven and that the lid fits tightly. I like to take my turkey and make slits in the breast so that when I pour on the butter solution that it penetrates the meat. This keeps the meat moist and gives it an even body taste. Never stuff your turkey before it is ready to cook. This can warm it up inside and cause bacteria to form if it is not put directly in the oven. If your turkey does not fit in your Dutch Oven, cut it in half and cook a half at a time. Stuff the turkey with sage dressing or chestnut stuffing found in the Log Cabin Grub cookbook Apple stuffing or, just put 3 or 4 sliced apples inside the bird to keep it moist.

BUTTER SEASONING OR BASTING

1/2 c. butter   1/2 tsp. Real salt
1/4 tsp pepper   1 tsp. Log Cabin seasoning
1 c. water   1/4 tsp onion salt
Combine all ingred. and warm to melt butter.
Pour over Turkey after it is in Dutch Oven.

DRESSING

Mouth watering

6 c. dried bread crumbs   1 tsp. salt
1/2 tsp. pepper   5 tbsp. sage
1 med. onion chopped   3 stocks celery chopped
8 eggs & enough water to moisten all ingredients.
Mix together and stuff the turkey. Use cream of chicken soup to mix the dressing. Left over rice and carrots can be added.

36

HOW ABOUT SOME GOURMET

NOW THIS IS A MEATBALL

1/2 c bread crumbs
2 lb. hamburger
1 1/4 tsp. salt
1/4 tsp. pepper
1 can beef broth (1 1/2 cups)
3 carrots, sliced
2 green peppers, sliced
1 c brown sugar

1/2 c minced onion
2 eggs
1 tsp. ginger
2 tbsp. oil
1 lb. fresh mushrooms
1/4 c vinegar
1/3 c corn starch
1/4 c soy sauce

12" Dutch Oven 350 degrees
12 briquettes in a Volcano,
10 bottom 15 to for briquettes only.
12 briquettes for Log Cabin pot
belly stove
350 degrees in you oven
"wait for the smell"

You can't hide this one from food lovers "

Combine bread, onion and 3/4 c. water. Add beef, eggs, salt, ginger & pepper. Make meatballs and cook in oil until brown. Pour off all fats. Put broth & 1 1/2 c. water in the Dutch Oven and heat. Add carrots and cook 15 minutes. Add mushrooms and green peppers. Cook until vegetables are tender. Remove meatballs and veggies, keep warm. Add brown sugar, vinegar and soy sauce to broth. Bring to a boil. Mix cornstarch in 1 c. water, add to broth mix. Mixture will turn clear and thick. Return meatballs and vegetables to broth. Serve over noodles or rice.

37

COWBOY RIBS HAWAIIAN STYLE

4 lbs. Boneless spareribs, cut
in 1 1/2 " strips
3/4 c cornstarch
1/4 c soy sauce
3/4 c water
1 1/2 c pineapple chunks (save the Juice)
(2 green peppers cut in chunks)

1/4 c molasses
1/2 c vinegar
3/4 c pineapple juice

12 or 14" Dutch Oven
350 degrees with 10 coals
bottom and 15 top

" Cook-em up, Serve em out "

In a warmed greased Dutch Oven, place the ribs. Combine cornstarch, molasses and soy sauce to make a paste. Spread paste on both sides of the ribs. Combine sugar, vinegar, water, pineapple juice and heat until sugar dissolves. Pour over ribs. Return the oven to heat and cook at 350 degrees for 50 to 60 minutes. The meat will begin to pull from the bone when done. The vinegar acts as a tenderizer but if the ribs are real meaty and big it will take longer to cook them. Add pineapple chunks and green peppers cubes. Recover and simmer for 5 minutes more. Serve with rice or buttered noodles. This will serve about 8 to 10 people

Sprinkling crust with powdered sugar, prevent them from going soggy with cream pies!

38

PORKY PINEAPPLE SPARERIBS

4 lbs. boneless pork spareribs
1/2 c flour   1 tsp. salt
1/4 tsp. pepper   ½ cup catsup
1/4 c molasses
1/4 c vinegar
1 lg onion chopped fine
1 lg green pepper
1 lg can chunk pineapple

12" Dutch Oven 350 Degrees

It takes awhile to cook - but its worth it.

I even like this one

Warm and oil your Dutch Oven. Put pineapple juice, vinegar, and seasoning in oven and simmer until bubbling. Put the ribs into the oven. Cover and cook at 350 for 50 minutes. Remove lid and stir ribs to baste with juices. Add ½ cup catsup and cook until ribs are tender, another 10 to 20 minutes. Add pineapple chunks, green pepper and onion. Return to heat for ten minutes to heat through. Great gourmet dish and excellent with Dutch Oven potatoes or rice.

THIS RECIPE IS ONE WE FELL ACROSS AT A BACK COUNTRY HORSE SHOW IN BOISE, IDAHO.

When you forget the sweet and sour sauce you make do with what you can. The rangers and the horse people never complained. Those horse people are some of the best.

RANCH HOUSE GOULASH ON STRAW (NOODLES).

1 lb. beef cut in cubes	2 medium onions chopped	12" Dutch Oven 350 Degrees
1/4 tsp. dry mustard	1-1/4 tsp. paprika	serves 8 to 10
2 tbsp. brown sugar	1-1/4 tsp. salt	
3 tbsp. Worcestershire sauce	3/4 tsp. vinegar	
6 tbsp. catsup	1-1/2 c water	
2 tbsp. flour	3 c noodles	

This Kind of Cookin will KEEP The rooster in the HEN House".

Roll meat in flour and brown in greased Dutch Oven. Add onion and sauté. Combine mustard, paprika, brown sugar and salt. In separate bowl combine Worcestershire sauce, vinegar, catsup and add to mustard mixture. Add to meat mixture and pour in 1 cup water. Stir and cover. Cook over low heat until meat is very tender, about 90 minutes. Blend 2 tbsp. of flour with 1/2 cup water and add to meat until it thickens as gravy. Boil noodles as package says or cook rice or make mashed potatoes. Serve meat over prepared dish.

VARIATION:
Omit catsup and add 1/2 c sour cream.

10 or 11 briquettes in Volcano – 10 bottom 15 top briquettes only – 325 degrees in your oven.

(" my Kind of Cookin "")

40

CORNBREAD AND CHILI PIE

Make your chili in your Dutch Oven, Using the recipe on page 27. Add a large can of corn and let the chili sit off the heat while you prepare the cornbread mixture. Leave the lid off so some of the heat will escape and not kill the baking powder action. The Cornbread recipe can be found in **LOG CABIN GRUB COOKBOOK** but for those who don't have my first book, the recipe is as follows:

2 c cornmeal   2-1/2 tsp baking powder
1 tsp. salt   3 tbsp. flour
2 c milk   3 eggs
2 tbsp. bacon grease or margarine or lard.

Mix all dry ingredients, pour in milk and mix lightly stir. Add eggs 1 at a time mixing after each. Add cooled grease, pour over chili and bake in Dutch Oven at 350 degrees for 25 minutes or until lightly browned.

" A Family Favorite "

LICKIN GOOD CHICKEN

1/4 c. cognac   8 slices Swiss cheese
1/2 c sour cream   1/2 c chopped parsley
4 chicken breasts, boned and skinned
1 can cream mushroom soup
3 tbsp. white wine or sherry
Melted butter
Stuffing mix or sage dressing page 36

Heat DUTCH OVEN and pour COGNAC in. Ignite, after flame goes out, place chicken breasts in the bottom and lay slice of cheese over each. Mix the soup with wine and sour cream, pour over chicken. Sprinkle with stuffing mix and drizzle melted butter over all. Cook in Dutch Oven at 350 degrees for 45 minutes. Chicken will be done and slightly brown. Serve with seasoned buttered wild rice or potatoes.

41

LOG CABIN ROLL-UPS

6 cube steaks or 3 lbs. sirloin cut in strips
12 strips bacon cut into pieces
1 large onion chopped fine
Dressing mix (optional)
Salt and pepper

Pound meat with cleaver or rolling pin to slightly flatten out. Spray with Vinegar mixture (4 to 1) to tenderize. Flour meat on one side and lay out on board or table. Flour side down. Salt and pepper up side of meat. Combine bacon and onion and place generous spoonfuls on each strip of meat. If desired, spread dressing over onion mixture. Roll up like a jellyroll and fasten each end with a toothpick or skewer. Brown rollups in hot shortening in a Dutch Oven. Add 1 cup of water and cover. Bake for 30 minutes and remove from heat. Arrange carrots and new red potatoes around the meat. Return to heat and bake 20 minutes more or until potatoes are soft. Flour from steak will make some gravy, but you can increase it by adding 3 tbsp. of cornstarch to a cup of water and pouring in the pot. You can remove roll-ups first or leave them in the gravy. Be creative and try different things. Add mixed vegetable only the last 15 minutes of cooking. Make extra gravy and serve with noodles. You could also add 1-cup sour cream to the gravy mixture just before serving.

12 or 11 briquettes in Volcano – 10 bottom 15 top briquettes only – 350 degrees in your

POTATOES AND VEGETABLES

This section will be on vegetables and potato dishes. Some will be for dinner, some for lunch and maybe you can try something different and switch them to breakfast. It's all in the pot. My mom always said " who decided what's for which meal"?. So be daring and try to be different.

OLD FASHIONED DUTCH OVEN POTATOES

6 slices bacon cut into bite size pieces
2 medium onions sliced
5 lbs. potatoes, sliced
1 c. chopped mushrooms
1 can cream mushroom soup
1 c. shredded cheddar cheese
(any combination of cheese can be used)

This is a good one for Potatoes.

12" Dutch Oven 350 Degrees
10 bottom & 15 top – Briquettes only

Warm Dutch Oven and cook bacon until almost done. Add onions and cook till lightly brown, dump in potato and stir together. Cover and cook till potatoes are almost done. About 20 to 25 minutes. Add Mushrooms cover and cook for 5 minutes. Add soup and cook for 5 minutes more heating all the way through. Remove from heat, spread cheese over the top, cover and let stand till cheese melts.

43

DUTCH OVEN POTATOES & ONIONS

1 lb. bacon cut into small pieces
12 potatoes   3 onions
1/2 c water   Salt & Pepper
While bacon is frying in a 12" Dutch Oven, peel, wash and slice potatoes and onions. Add potatoes and onions to bacon grease and stir to coat with grease. Pour water in and salt and pepper to taste. Bake for 45 minutes at 350 degrees. HINT: You can add a can of beer and omit the water for a new and different flavor. if you wish, sprinkle cheese on top the last 5 minutes of cooking time.
VARIATIONS:
1 cup shredded carrots
1 cup chopped celery
1 cup mushrooms

" Bet ya can't eat Just ONE!"

YUMMIE POTATOES

24 oz pkg. of hash browns
1 can cream chicken soup
1 c sour cream
1 c grated cheese
1/2 c chopped green onion
1/2 c melted butter

Mix all ingredients together in a greased warm DUTCH OVEN. Top the mixture with 2 cups crushed corn flakes and 2 tbsp. melted butter. Bake at 325 degrees in a 12" DUTCH OVEN until the cheese is melted through. About 30 minutes.
10 briquettes in Volcano – 10 bottom 15 top briquettes only – 325 degrees in your

" Just give em a try partner"

44

DUTCH OVEN GARDEN SKILLET

6 zucchini small, sliced
3 med. tomatoes
1 medium cauliflower separated
1 chopped green pepper
1 medium sliced onion
1 tsp garlic   salt and pepper
1 c mushrooms cut in half

This one will trip your trigger"

Grease the DUTCH OVEN and melt 1/4 c butter, margarine or shortening. Put in all ingredients and sauté for 3 or 4 minutes. Add 3 tomatoes and cover. Cook for 15 min. Sprinkle with parmesan cheese and serve..
White Cheese works well also

REMEMBER THE ONLY WAT YOU DRY CAST IRON IS TO HEAT IT ON THE FIRE TO DRY OUT THE MOISTURE.

FROSTED VEGETABLES

4 cups vegetables(broccoli-carrots-cauliflower-etc.)	
1/2 c mayonnaise	1/4 tsp. salt
1 tsp. mustard	3/4 c shredded cheese
1/4 tsp. paprika	1/4 tsp. pepper

Wash and slice vegetables. Place in a greased DUTCH OVEN. Put in 1/2 c water and steam at 350 degrees for 15 minutes. Remove from heat and add mixture of mayonnaise, mustard, salt and pepper. Spread cheese on top and cover. Cook for 5 to 10 minutes until cheese is melted. Sprinkle with paprika & serve
HINT: Add onions, celery or garlic for flavor.
12 briquettes in Volcano
10 bottom 12 top briquettes only

45

CRUMMY GREEN BEANS

5 tbsp. butter	6 tbsp. flour
1/2 tsp. salt	1/4 tsp. pepper
2 c milk	2 c green beans drained
1/2 c grated cheese	1 tbsp. Onion Powder
2 tbsp. butter	1/2 c bread crumbs

Melt 5 tbsp. of butter in a 12" Dutch Oven. Stir in flour, salt and pepper. Slowly add milk and stir until mixture thickens. Fold in green beans and spread cheese over the top. Melt 2 tbsp. Of butter in a separate pan and stir in breadcrumbs. Spread over the cheese and bake at 350 for 20 to 25 minutes. Serves 4 to 6 people
10 briquettes in Volcano – 10 bottom 12 top briquettes only

BEAN AND FRENCH ONION

2 large cans green beans
1 can cream mushroom soup
1 can French onion rings

Drain green beans and place in greased Dutch Oven. 10" will do. Add cream of mushroom soup. Mix well. Sprinkle onion rings on top. Bake at 325 for 25 min. or until bubbly and hot. This has an excellent taste and serves good with a meat dish. 9 briquettes in Volcano – 8 bottom 10 top briquettes only

— These will keep your well "pumpin water"

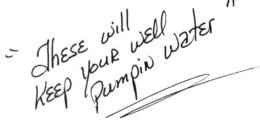

46

ZUCCHINI & TOMATOES

4 medium zucchini sliced
1/2 c chopped onion
1/4 c chopped celery
1-16 oz can stewed tomatoes
1 tsp. salad herbs or Italian dressing

Place tomatoes, herbs, onion, celery & zucchini in a greased 10" DUTCH OVEN. Add ½ c water. Place over heat & bake for 20 minutes. Remove from heat when veggies are soft and sprinkle with parmesan cheese. Serve warm. 350 degrees in your oven. 10 briquettes in Volcano 8 bottom and 11 top for briquettes only.

Lock your car or neighbors will fill it with zucchini

ZUCCHINI CASSEROLE

2 zucchini sliced	1/2 green pepper
1 can creamed corn	1 egg
1 lg chopped onion	2 tsp. garlic salt
1/2 c cracker crumbs	salt & pepper

Beat eggs in a shallow bowl, dip onion, place zucchini & green pepper in egg. Roll in cracker crumbs. Melt 2-tbsp. oil in 10" DUTCH OVEN. Fry veggies until light brown & turn. Sprinkle garlic on top and pour in corn. Bake for 25 minutes over medium heat, enough to heat through. Serve with meat dish. 350 degrees in your oven. Wait for the smell

I LOVE THE TASTE THAT BACON GREASE GIVES TO DUTCH OVEN FOOD. I ALWAYS SAVE MINE IN A GLASS JAR & REFRIGERATE.

47

GOURMET TWICE BAKED POTATOES

4 medium size potatoes
14 mushrooms sliced
1/2 c butter
1 tsp salt
1 cup white or mixed grated cheeses

1 head of broccoli
2 tbsp. Minced onion
¾ c cream
½ tsp. pepper

"Add a little chili to the mix before adding back to potatoes"

Early in the day, bake the potatoes. Set aside to cool. Melt butter in a 12 " DUTCH OVEN, sauté onions and add mushrooms, cook until tender. Set aside. Wash Broccoli, chop to desired size and steam till tender. Remove from heat and rinse in cold water to stop the cooking process. Set aside. Split potatoes in half and carefully remove the insides to a bowl with butter, cream, salt and pepper. Whip till fluffy, layer potatoes with mushroom mixture and broccoli in the potato shells. Top with cheese and paprika. Return to oven, heat on medium until warm. Sprinkle cheese over top and melt in oven.

VARIATIONS:
Try alternating potato with chili instead of broccoli.
Put creamed chunks of chicken with broccoli.
Put pieces of chipped beef with potato
Try a layer of chili in potato
Add corn flakes to potato mixture or crumble on top

Worth every minute it takes to cook em!!

DUTCH OVEN POTATOES BY DON

6 large potatoes, sliced
1 square butter(1/2 c butter)
2 medium onions (chopped)
1/2 cup salsa
1 can cheddar cheese soup
2 tbsp. Log Cabin Seasoning
salt & pepper to taste

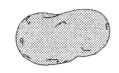

Grease a 12" Dutch Oven and arrange 1/4 of the onions in the bottom. Put sliced potatoes on the onions, sprinkle seasoning on top. Mix salsa and soup with 1/2 can water. Pour 1/4 of mixture over potatoes. Repeat and use up all potatoes & onions, ending with soup and salsa mixture. You can sprinkle chopped green onions or broccoli on top for color. Cook in your Volcano with 10 briquettes or follow the cooking instructions on page 9 for 25 minutes.

One of the nicest guys in Idaho gave me this recipe

CHICKEN FRIED ZUCCHINI

2 medium thinly sliced zucchini
2 eggs
1/4 cup milk
1 cup bread crumbs
2 tbsp. Log Cabin Seasoning
2 medium onions thinly sliced
1 tbsp. garlic powder
salt & pepper to taste

Here's another Roll up your window recipe

Grease a 12" Dutch Oven and put zucchini & onions in the pot. Mix eggs, milk & seasoning, pour over the zucchini. Pour breadcrumbs over the top and lightly toss with a fork. Cook for 20 to 25 minutes at 360. Stir once or twice to help brown crumbs. This can be fried on grill or fry pan also.

49

DUTCH POTATO SPEARS

6 large baking potatoes
1/2 c. butter
1/4 c parmesan cheese
1 tsp. garlic powder
salt & pepper

"Snowbird Special"

Slice potatoes in quarters length wise. Place in 12" DUCH OVEN, skin down. Melt butter and pour over potatoes. Sprinkle with parmesan, garlic, salt and pepper. Can put a dash of paprika & parsley if you want a little color. Bake for 25 minutes at 350 degrees and remember the 2/3 rule. In your Volcano use only 10 Briquettes.

GRANDMAS GREEN TOMATO STEW

1 medium onion diced
3 medium potatoes diced
3 medium green tomatoes diced
4 tbsp. butter
1/2 c water

Sauté onions in butter and add remaining ingredients. Salt and pepper to taste. You can add some celery, a touch of garlic salt, mushrooms, a pinch of cumin, or use your imagination to e creative. This is a great basic stew. Bake in DUTCH Oven 25 minutes at 350 degrees. In your Volcano use only 10 briquettes.

HEATING YOUR DUTCH OVEN TO EVAPORATE THE MOISTURE IS THE ONLY WAT TO DRY IT.

BREADS ROLLS
BISCUITS AND
MORE

Your Oven Or
Dutch Oven

BREADS, ROLLS, BISCUITS AND MUFFINS

"Man cannot live by bread alone But a D.O. Bread can almost change your mind."

      The word bread, seems to apply to the same old monotonous thing that is served at every meal. We often take bread for granted that it will be there and it's usually the same old white or wheat slice. No change, no glamour, all slices of equal size and isn't that exciting. Likely as not it is served on the same old plate. So-----try some of the following in your oven or a Dutch Oven to spruce up your meal. Go out on a limb and *"leaf"* your family wanting more. For dinner, try adding a hot bread of roll and you'll find that you will have more meat servings to go around because your family ate extra bread.

BASIC DUTCH OVEN BREAD

3 c flour
1 tbsp. baking powder
1 tsp. salt
enough water to make a dough
Mix dry ingredients with 3 tbsp. water to start. Add more if necessary. Work as little as possible and bake in a greased Dutch Oven for 20 to 25 min. It can be bake as one large loaf or several small.

VARIATIONS:
Milk instead of water
1 tbsp. sugar
1 egg
1 tbsp. oil
1 tsp. cinnamon or nutmeg
Raisins, currents, drained blueberries, Cheeses,
Garlic, onions and more. All to make your bread taste swell.

The Taste is outrageous

52

INDIAN FRY BREAD

3 c flour
4 tsp. baking powder
3 tsp. salt
2 tbsp. sugar
1-1/4 c lukewarm water

Mix all ingredients together. Add liquid all at once. Mix to biscuit stage. Roll out flat, cut into squares and let stand for 5 minutes. Fry in hot grease in a 10" DUTCH OVEN. Will taste and look like our scones of today. The less you handle the dough, the better.

ALL PURPOSE BAKING MIX

2 c flour   4 tsp. baking powder
1/4 tsp. salt   1/2 tsp. cream tarter
1 tbsp. sugar   1/2 c Crisco

Use it often

Mix all dry ingredients together and sift 2 or 3 times. Place in a covered container and use as needed. Add Crisco and 3/4 c water or milk to mix as dough. If you prefer to use buttermilk, also ad 1/2 tsp. soda. Its a mix to keep on hand for easy biscuits for a meal. They can be dropped by tsp. in a greased DUTCH Oven, and baked at 350 using the 2/3 rule.

ADD 1 TBSP APPLE CIDER VINEGAR TO YOUR BREAD MIXTURE TO PREVENT MOLDING

Get the Butter & Jelly Ready - or Eat it plain.

53

SHEEPHERDER BREAD

5 tsp. yeast
3 c lukewarm water
2 1/2 tsp. salt
1/4 c sugar
7 1/2 c flour

= Oh the splender of it all"

Into a room temperature large bowl, put yeast, salt, sugar and water. Stir in yeast until it is dissolved. Cover and let the spores bubble for a few minutes. Pour in 6 cups of the flour and stir until blended to a dough. Sprinkle flour over the dough and dump out on a floured surface. Add the remaining flour of 1 cup, and kneed until good bread consistency. Put into a greased bowl and cover with a wet towel. Let it rise until double in size. Punch down and shape into 2 loafs. Grease a 10 or 12" Dutch Oven and cover with a lid. Let rise again. Bake at 350 for 35 or 40 minutes. Bread will turn golden brown. Remember your 2/3 rule and don't burn the bottom.

IF YOU ONLY WANT TO BAKE PART OF YOUR DOUGH, FREEZE IT BEFORE IT RISES THE 1ST TIME. WHEN YOU ARE READY, REMOVE IT, LET IT THAW AND RAISE. BAKE AS USUAL.

OLD FASHIONED POTATO ROLLS

1-1/2 c warm water	2/3 cup sugar
1 pkg. dry yeast	2/3 c left over mashed potatoes or instant potatoes
2/3 c hot water	1-1/2 tsp. salt
2/3 c soft shortening	2 eggs
7 to 7 1/2 c flour	

Don't be afraid to share this - It will make good friends.

Mix 1 1/2 cups warm water in a large mixing bowl. Sprinkle the yeast on top and set aside to let soften. Mix potatoes with hot but not boiling water and set aside. When yeast is dissolved, add salt, shortening, eggs and cooled potatoes. Mix well and add 2 cups of the flour. Beat until mixture is smooth. Cover with the towel and let mixture rest 10 minutes. Mix in remaining flour until the dough is easy to handle. Turn out onto a lightly floured surface and knead until smooth and elastic. Place in a greased bowl and turn so that the grease will cover the dough. Cover with a damp cloth and let rise until double. This will take about 1-1/2 to 2 hours. Shape into rolls and place in 12 " Dutch oven. Be sure that the oven is greased well. Cover and let rise again. Place oven over heat and remember to put more on top that the bottom. bread requires baking temperatures and only small amount of heat on bottom. After 10 minutes, remove lid to see if rolls are browning and pulling from the sides. Makes 4 dozen.

*Easy to make --- Easy to Eat ---
Hard to Leave any for others"*

NEVADA BREAD BASQUE STYLE
(This recipe won 1st place at Nevada Fair)

Speech bubble: DON'T BURY ME WITHOUT MY BREAD

Yield; 1 very large loaf -- serves 15 - 20 people
Preparation Time 45 minutes

3 c very hot water	1/2 c butter, margarine or shortening
1/2 c sugar	2 1/2 tsp. salt
2 pkgs. dry yeast(4 tsp.)	1/4 c oil
9 1/2 c flour	

Baking time 45 minutes at 350 degrees.

In a sauce pan, combine hot water, butter sugar and salt. Stir until the butter melts. let cool to 115 degrees. Transfer to a large mixing bowl. Stir in yeast and cover. Set in a warm place until spores begin to bubble. About 15 minutes. Add 5 cups of flour and beat with a heavy duty mixer or by hand to form a thick batter. Work in with your hands or a large wooden spoon, enough flour to form a stiff dough. Turn out on a floured board and knead it smooth. Add flour as needed to prevent sticking. Put dough into a greased bowl and cover. Let rise till double in size. about 1 1/2 hours. Punch down and knead again on a floured board to form a smooth ball. Dough maybe divided into two pieces, other wise it takes a 20 " Dutch oven to cook it.

a TRIED & TRUE RECIPE

continued next page.

56

NEVADA BASQUE BREAD CONT:

You can cut a tin foil circle to cover the bottom of the oven if you wish. Grease the inside of the Oven thoroughly and the lid. Let bread rise until double and it may push the lid off your 12" oven. Bake cover with lid at 350 to 375 degrees for 12 minutes. Loaf will turn brown and sound hollow when done. Remove from the oven and turn on to cooling rack. It may be quite heavy, so you may need help to do this. The Basque Sheepherder always cut a cross in the top of their bread before they bake it, and then always gave the first piece to their dogs. Dogs were very important to the herders and bread was the staff of life.

TURN MEAT WITH TONGS NOT A FORK, IT PIERCES THE MEAT AND LET THE JUICES OUT.

CRUSH SWEETENED CEREAL OR STALE DONUTS AND USE FOR TOPPING ON MUFFINS.

SPRINKLE SALT IN THE BOTTOM OF PAN BEFORE COOKING OATMEAL, IN HELPS PREVENT STICKING.

USE AN ICE CREAM SCOOP TO FILL YOUR MUFFIN PANS OR CUPCAKE PAPERS, ITS JUST RIGHT.

It don't get any BETTER.

CINNAMON ROLLS MADE EASY

Thaw 1 loaf of frozen bread dough
1 -12" Dutch Oven
1/4 c butter
1/2 c brown sugar
1 c cream or milk (preferably whipping cream

1 c chopped nuts
1/4 tsp. nutmeg
Cinnamon &sugar.

10 briquettes in Volcano
10 briquettes bottom – 15 top for briquettes only. Coals around bottom outside edge only.

Roll out bread dough to oblong shape on floured board. Butter top and sprinkle with cinnamon and sugar to lightly cover. You can also sprinkle on raisins if you like. Roll up from side and cut about 1" thick. In bottom of 12" Oven, grease and pour the cream or milk. Sprinkle brown sugar around the pan and add nuts and nutmeg. Arrange the rolls touching each other in the entire pan. Squeeze them in if necessary. Let the rolls rise to almost double their size, about 1 hour. Cover and bake at 350 for 35 minutes. Remember to use the 2/3 ruling and more heat on top than the bottom. Rolls will brown slightly on top and pull from the sides when done. Mix 1/2 cup powdered sugar with milk to a thin consistency and dribble over the top. Eat warm and enjoy.

REMEMBER MILK BURNS EASILY, KEEP HEAT LOW ON BOTTOM IN A CIRCLE AROUND THE OUTSIDE EDGE OF OVEN.

This one will keep the home fires Burning"

58

QUICK CHUCKWAGON WHEAT BREAD

2 c wheat flour   1 tsp. soda
2 c buttermilk   1 tsp. salt
3 tbsp. molasses or honey
1 tsp. baking powder.
1/2 c raisins   1 egg beaten
1 1/2 tbsp. butter

Combine egg, buttermilk, molasses & melted butter. Stir in dry ingredients that have been mixed together. Stir in raisins, and spoon batter in to.2 greased loaf pans. Pans can be baked in 14" Dutch Oven, by placing few rocks in the bottom to set the pans on, the rocks must be flat and even. Bake in 12" Dutch oven at 400 degrees for 1 hour. Can be baked as 2 loaves or as biscuits in a warmed & oiled Dutch Oven. No need for loaf pans.

COWBOY CORN DINNER ROLLS

Boil together: 2 c water, 1/2 c corn 6 Tbsp. sugar & 2 tsp. sugar. Cook over low heat until thick. Add 1/2 c margarine. Remove from heat. Cool to Luke warm. Add 1/2 c warm water. Add 2/3 c powdered milk, 2 tbsp. milk, & 2 eggs. Put in a large bowl. Mix in 4 cups flour, mix for 10 minutes. Let rise until double in bulk. Roll and shape into rolls. Rise to double and bake in greased Dutch Oven at 350 for 12 minutes or wait for the smell. 10 briquettes on bottom 15 on top. 10 briquettes on the volcano. Remember to wait for the smell. I will tell you when it's done.
10 briquettes in Volcano or 10 bottom 14 top briquettes only. 350 in your home oven.

Remember "Dutch Oven Cooks Keep Em Hot"

59

WESTERN FRENCH BREAD

3 c warm water	3 tsp. salt
2 tbsp. sugar	7 cup flour
2 tbsp. shortening	canned milk
2 tbsp. dry yeast	Sesame seeds (optional)

("We caught this Bread Loafin")

Combine water, sugar, shortening, salt & yeast. Mix until yeast is dissolved and add flour. Make a good pliable dough. Let rise about 1 hour and divide into 3 loafs. Divide and bake in 2 warm greased 12" Dutch Ovens and brush with canned milk.

Sprinkle with sesame seeds if desired and let rise 1 hour. Brush with canned milk lightly again and bake for 30 minutes at 350 degrees. Bread will be a golden brown. Remember the 2/3 rule and do not put too much heat on the bottom. No more than 10 bottom heat.

NO MATTER HOW THEY DRESS IT UP, UPON THE GROCERS SHELF.
NO BREAD CAN EVER BE AS GOOD AS WHAT YOU BAKE YOURSELF.

Bury me not on the Lone Prairie unless you bring my Bread!

60

GINGERBREAD

Yesterday's Recipe for today's Cooks.

1/2 c butter	1 cup sugar
2 eggs	1/2 c molasses
1/4 c honey	2-1/2 c flour
1/2 tsp. salt	2 tsp. ginger
2 tsp. baking powder	

In a 12" Dutch Oven grease and warm it slightly. Cream butter and add sugar. Beat until light & fluffy. Add eggs, beat well. Mix 3/4 c boiling water, molasses and honey. Blend well. Mix together flour, soda, salt & ginger. Add to creamed mixture, then add honey mixture & combine well. Pour into Dutch Oven and bake for 35 minutes or until done. Will pull from sides of Oven. Serve warm with whipped cream. Low bottom heat

SOUR CREAM COFFEE CAKE

"Great for Company"

3/4 c butter	1 tsp. baking powder
2 c sugar	1/2 tsp. salt
2 eggs	1 c sour cream
2 c flour	1 tsp. vanilla

Cream butter & sugar. Add eggs & beat well. Blend in vanilla. Add flour, baking powder & salt. Blend in sour cream. Pour 1/2 the batter in a greased 10"Dutch Oven. Sprinkle with Brown sugar, cinnamon & chopped nuts. Add remaining batter and bake at 350 degrees for about 1 hour. The smell or pulling from side of pan will tell you when it is done. Glaze with Powdered sugar, Vanilla &milk mixture.

The smell from both of these cakes will tell you when they are done.
50 briquettes should cook the ginger bread and 50 the coffee cake for briquettes only 10 bottom 12 top
12 or less briquette in your Volcano and the Log Cabin Pot Belly

61

DREAM TRAIL BISCUITS

2 C cake or white flour sifted
1 tsp. Salt
3 tsp. baking powder   1
c heavy cream whipped

Keep them Biscuits Coming Partner"

Mix all dry ingredients together and fold into whipped cream. Pat
out softly in 12" greased DUTCH OVEN. Cut into shapes and cover. Bake at 450 degrees (hot) until lightly brown.
About 12 minutes. Quick and easy biscuit for a fast supper or morning breakfast with jam. Great with sausage
gravy. If you want to substitute sour dough, ½ cup will do and omit the baking powder!

**WE MAY LIVE WITH FRIENDS, WE MAY LIVE WITHOUT BOOKS,
BUT CIVILIZED MAN CANNOT LIVE WITHOUT COOKS.**

Caution
Dutch Oven Cooks can
go from 0 to 350 in 6 to
10 minutes with a
Volcano

62

CORN BREAD DUTCH OVEN STYLE

1/2 c flour
1-1/2 c corn meal
1/2 tsp. baking soda
3 tsp. baking powder
1 tsp. salt

2 eggs
1 c buttermilk *
1 tbsp. molasses
1/4 c shortening-oil or margarine

"This will tempt your pallet"

Ummm

*1 cup milk & 3 tbsp. powdered buttermilk can be substituted) (1 tbsp. sugar for molasses) Put all dry ingredients in a bowl and make a well in the middle. Add all the other wet ingredients and mix together well. Place in a greased 12' DUTCH OVEN and bake at 350 degrees for 35 minutes

THE 3 MAIN WAYS TO CHECK DONENESS ON A BREAD OR CAKE RECIPE IS --PULL FROM SIDES OF PAN-- STRAW OR TOOTHPICK WILL PULL OUT CLEAN---TOP WILL NOT INDENT WHEN TOUCHED.

TRY BAKING CORN BREAD ON TOP OF CHILI IN YOUR DUTCH OVEN FOR CHILI PIE. SPOON IT ON THE LAST 10 OR 15 MINUTES – IT WILL TELL YOU WHEN IT'S DONE

CHUCKWAGON BISCUITS

Did you know that covered wagons traveled an average of 7 miles per day on their journey westward?

1 c. buttermilk   1 ½ tsp. Tsp. soda
(1 c. sourdough starter(page 43 Log Cabin Grub)
)2 c flour   1/3 c milk
1/2 c butter   2 tsp. baking powder
1 tsp. Real salt   1/2 tsp. Sugar, honey, or molasses Optional

Mix all ingredients together and turn out on a floured board. Pat the mixture flat on board. Cut out biscuits according to the size you want. Cut in squares, use round coffee cup or glass, tin clean tuna can, cookie cutter or etc. After cutting most of the dough into shapes, make any shape of biscuit you want. Do not work dough over and over, it becomes hard and crusty. Try to cut most all of the biscuits out of 1st two times . Arrange in 12" DUTCH OVEN and bake at about 350 degrees for 20 to 25 minutes. Be sure to grease D.O. before using, and bacon grease gives it a great taste. See Page 9 for temperature settings. The sugar will calm down the sourdough taste some. Brush tops of biscuits with milk for a faster golden brown color. Remove from oven and dust tops with butter or grease if desired. 10 briquettes in Volcano – 10 bottom 15 top briquettes only. The smell will tell you when it is done.

Nobody knows what a man can do, until they walk a mile in his moccasins (Yesterday's history, tomorrow is a mystery, today is a gift from God)

Thanks to the Pioneers for today's world!

64

MOUNTAIN MUFFINS

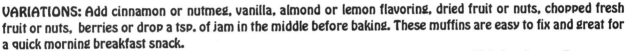

1-3/4 c flour
3 tbsp. sugar
1 tsp. baking powder
3/4 c buttermilk**
6 tbsp. lard, oil or shortening
2 eggs beaten

**3/4 c milk with 2 tbsp. powdered
  buttermilk can be substituted.
3/4 tsp. salt

Put all dry ingredients in a mixing bowl, Stir to combine and add milk, egg & lard. Mix well & drop by heaping tbsp. in a greased 12" DUTCH OVEN, 20 to 25 minutes @ 375.

VARIATIONS: Add cinnamon or nutmeg, vanilla, almond or lemon flavoring, dried fruit or nuts, chopped fresh fruit or nuts, berries or drop a tsp. of jam in the middle before baking. These muffins are easy to fix and great for a quick morning breakfast snack.
10 briquettes in your Volcano or 10 bottom 15 top briquettes only. 350 in your oven. Wait for the smell.

TRY A BLOCK PARTY WITH YOUR NEIGHBORS USING YOU DUTCH OVENS.
DUTCH OVENERS HAVE MORE FIRIENDS

65

NUMBER #1 TRAIL BREAD

2 c *fluffed flour   1 level tsp. salt
1/4 c bacon grease, shortening or butter
1 level tbsp. baking powder
1 c milk

TO MIX: Combine all dry ingredients in a pan or bowl, then with fork or your fingers, work the fat into the flour mixture only until it appears to be like a coarse cornmeal. Pour milk and egg into the mix and stir only enough to take up the moisture.

TO BAKE: Grease the DUTCH OVEN liberally and dump the dough into the warmed oven. Spread the dough out in the pan. Smear grease on the top of the bread and bake. Can e covered and baked in the Dutch oven for 20 to 25 minutes at 350 degrees, Texture is like a fry bread. Can be flipped over after 15 minutes of baking

VARIATION: Add 1/4 c sugar to the dough.
*FLUFFED: Toss the flour with a fork to get the air back in the flour before measuring.
BANNOCK: The name given bread that was fried instead of baked in an oven.

"Heat em up to dry em"

The smell

66

DESSERTS & MORE

We sing the praise of Dutch Oven Cooking

Starting on Page 67

CAKES & PIE

THIS IS THE SWEET SECTION.. **OHHHHHHHHHHH** SO GOOD

"a Little History"

HISTORIC TIES-   APRON STRINGS

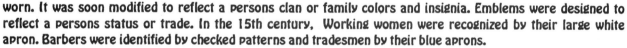

When Eve was tempted in the garden of Eden and her and Adam realized they were naked, the very first Apron was hers. Thus from good misfortune did some good come. In the middle ages in Europe the custom arose of using a precious piece of cloth to cover their clothes. Soon all women were draping cloth across their lap at meal time. Then cloth was tied around their waist to protect their skirts all day. The word apron comes from the French word NAPERON which means napkin. From the 13th century on, aprons were worn. It was soon modified to reflect a persons clan or family colors and insignia. Emblems were designed to reflect a persons status or trade. In the 15th century, Working women were recognized by their large white apron. Barbers were identified by checked patterns and tradesmen by their blue aprons.

In the late 16th century, upper class women began to wear lace and fine linen aprons that were useless, to identify their class. In the next century, working people wore flannel or canvas. Farmers wives wore brown, blue, or checked aprons. Upper class people went to taffeta, silk and brocade. The fancier the better. Their help wore trimmed white upstairs and the lower floor wore black. The 17th and 18th century saw many changes. Fancy needlework, stripes, plaids and new brighter colors. Some long, some short, some full length and with bibs. The apron of today hangs mostly in the closet, but is a part of history.

67

OLD SPOTTED DOG PUDDING

I think it's named after me.

1 c brown sugar	1/2 c water
4 c toasted bread crumbs	1/2 c raisins
1 c peeled diced apples	1/4 c butter
2 eggs	1 1/2 c milk
1 tsp. cinnamon	1/4 tsp. nutmeg

In a sauce pan, combine water and sugar, bring to a boil and cook till thick and syrupy. (5 minutes) let cool. Warm and grease a 10" Dutch oven. Layer 1/2 the bread crumbs, syrup, apples and raisins in bottom or pan. Repeat till all ingredients are in pan. Pour butter over top and set aside. Mix eggs, milk cinnamon & nutmeg together and pour over bread mixture. Bake 35 minutes at 350 degrees. Sprinkle white cheese over the top. Allow time to cool (10 min.) and cut into servings. In today's world we can serve with Ice Cream, Yogurt or whip cream.

EARLY MOUNTAINMEN AND TRAVELERS NAMED THIS PUDDING BECAUSE OF THE RAISINS IN IT.

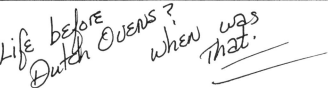

Life before Dutch Ovens? when was that.

ZUCCHINI BROWNIES

So Little Time, So much Food.

2 c flour	1-1/2 c sugar
1/4 c cocoa	1 tsp., salt
3/4 tsp. soda	1/2 c oil
2 tsp. vanilla	2 c grated zucchini

Mix all dry ingredients together. Add oil vanilla and grated zucchini to the dry ingredients. Put in 12" Dutch Oven that has been warmed and oiled. Bake at 350 degrees for 20 to 25 minutes. Sprinkle with powdered sugar when cool. Remember the 2/3 rule and more heat on top if using briquettes only. 10 briquettes in Volcano

Always more heat on top and less on the bottom when using briquettes!
When baking in your oven, just put on 350 degrees and wait for the smell!

DOING NOTHING IS THE MOST TIRESOME JOB IN THE WORLD, CAUSE ITS IMPOSSIBLE TO QUIT AND TAKE A REST.

QUICK TRAIL CINNAMON ROLLS

In a 12" Dutch Oven, pour 1/2 pt whipping cream or 1/2 cup (small can) condensed milk. Spread 1/2 cup Brown sugar around on milk and sprinkle with nuts. Place 15 or more rolls around on the cream, sugar mix. Bake with lid on for 18 to 22 minutes or wait for the smell. Turn the pan upside down and serve off the lid. A Carmel sauce will form. A thin glaze of powdered sugar frosting can be drizzled over the top while warm. If using frozen yeast rolls be sure to let rise to double size before baking.

10 to 12 briquettes in Volcano – no center heat. 10 bottom 15 top briquettes only.

Everyone's Favorite

69

CRISPY COUNTRY APPLES

"Oh Yeah"

12 large apples or 1 gallon canned apple
1/2 c sugar   1 tsp. cinnamon
3/4 c butter   1-1/2 c brown sugar
1 c flour   3/4 c oatmeal or granola

Peel the apples, slice and place in a warmed greased 12" Dutch Oven. Sprinkle sugar and cinnamon over the top. Combine the butter, flour, brown sugar and oatmeal. Spread over the top of the apples. Bake at 350 degrees for 35 to 40 minutes. Apples will be soft and golden brown. if you use canned apples, cook only 20 min.
10 briquettes on volcano
10 bottom 15 top briquettes only

ZUCCHINI CAKE

"Thank you Lord for good food."

3 eggs   1 cup oil
2 1/2 c sugar   3 tsp. vanilla
1 tsp. salt   1 tsp. soda
1 tsp. cinnamon   1/4 tsp. baking powder
3 c flour   2 c grated zucchini
1 c nuts

Combine eggs, oil, and vanilla and beat thoroughly Add dry ingredients and blend well. Stir in Zucchini and nuts. Bake in Dutch Oven for about 1 hour at 325 degrees. 2/3 rule check after 40 minutes. When done will pull from the sides. The smell will tell you when it's done. 10 briquettes in Volcano

REMEMBER EVERY TIME YOU LIFT THE LID ON A DUTCH OVEN, YOU DROP YOUR TEMPERATURE 35 TO 40 DEGREES & LOSE FOOD NUTRIENTS AND FLAVOR

"Dutch Oven Cooking - A way to turn a man's head by his stomach."

70

PIONEER CARROT CAKE

2 c flour	2 tsp. soda
2 tsp. cinnamon	1/2 tsp. salt
2 tsp. vanilla	1 c crushed pineapple drained
2 c grated carrots	1 1/2 c flaked coconut (optional)
1 c chopped nuts	3 eggs
3/4 c vegetable oil	3/4 c sugar-- 1/2 c. buttermilk

"This Recipe is a Company Pleaser"

Sift together first 4 ingredients, set aside. Beat eggs and add oil, buttermilk, sugar and vanilla. Mix well. Add flour mixture, pineapple, carrots, coconut (optional) and nuts. Pour Batter into a warm and greased Oven and bake for about 55 minutes or until you can smell it. A toothpick will come out clean when inserted. Cake will pull from sides of pan.
Cream Cheese Frosting; 3 c powdered sugar, 12 oz cream cheese, 1 tsp. milk and 1 tsp. vanilla mixed together well.

ADDING A PINCH OF BAKING POWDER TO POWDERED SUGAR FROSTINGS WILL HELP IT STAY MOIST AND NOT CRACK.

" Watch for the Cake Sheriff"

71

COYOTE DUTCH OVEN BROWNIES

1/2 c margarine   1 tbsp. milk
1 egg   1 c brown sugar
1 c flour   1/2 tsp. baking powder
1/8 tsp. salt   1/2 c nuts

Warm and oil 12" Dutch Oven. Melt butter and stir in sugar, and add egg and stir or whip until blended. Stir in remaining ingredients and mix well. Sprinkle with nuts and cover. Bake for 25 to 30. Brownies will pull from the sides of the pan when they are done. Frost immediately with chocolate or vanilla frosting. Great for an around the campfire snack. Don't forget the 2/3 rule.
More heat on top only when cooking with briquettes. Use 10 to 11 briquettes in a volcano

<u>A QUICK FROSTING CAN BE MADE BY ADDING A COUPLE DROPS OF</u>
<u>CHOCOLATE TO A PREPARED WHIPPED TOPPING.</u>

when you smell it, its ready.

72

E-Z BAR FRUIT COBBLER

Preheat Dutch Oven and lid. Melt ½ c margarine in the oven. Add a quart of fruit or a large can of fruit pie filling. Sprinkle a white cake mix over the top of fruit, and sprinkle a touch of cinnamon & sugar over the cake mix. Cover and cook for 25 min. or wait for the smell. 12" Dutch Oven.

10 bottom 15 top briquettes only
12 briquettes Volcano
Variations:
Peaches – White Cake Mix & 1 can Sprite or 1-Up
Cherries – Chocolate Cake Mix & 1 can Coke
Apple Spice Cake Mix & 1 Can Rootbeer
Can Cranberries and White Cake Mix & 1 Can Cream Soda
WHEN FIXING A FIRE FOR BAKING COBBLERS AND ETC., MOST OF THE HEAT
MUST BE ON THE TOP. NO HEAT UNDERNEATH ALWAYS AROUND THE OUTSIDE EDGES.

RICE PUDDING IN A HURRY

Take 2 c water and 1 c rice, put in a warmed oiled Dutch Oven and boil for 7 minutes. Then add;1-quart milk & 1/2 c butter. When the mixture is steamy, cover and simmer for 20 to 30 minutes. Beat 2 eggs well, add 1/2 c sugar, 1tsp. Cinnamon, 1-tsp. vanilla and 1 c raisins. Remove rice from heat and pour sugar mixture in, mix well and let stand covered 15 to 20 minutes. Serve.

"Never any leftovers here"

73

FRESH MOUNTAIN COBBLER

1/2 c sugar
1 tbsp. cornstarch
4 c fruit (Blueberries-cherries-apples-peaches-etc.,)
1 tsp. lemon juice

In a medium saucepan, blend sugar & cornstarch. Stir in fruit & lemon juice. Cook stirring often until mixture comes to boil and goes thick. remove from fire & cool while you prepare crust.

FOR A VARIETY, SPRINKLE CINNAMON & SUGAR ON TOP OF COBBLER MIX.

COBBLER CRUST

4 tbsp. sugar
1-1/2 tsp. baking powder
1/2 tsp. salt
1 c flour
3 tbsp. Butter softened or melted
2/3 c milk or cream

Measure flour, salt, baking powder & sugar in bowl. Cut butter into the mixture until it forms dough ball. Stir in cream, spoon on the hot fruit. Bake until the topping is golden brown. About 25 minutes.. Serve warm with whipped cream or Ice Cream.

" You won't have any trouble sharing these"

A DUTCH OVEN IS THE BEST WAY TO COOK A COBBLER. THE HEAT IS EVEN AND YOU CAN ADD BROWN SUGAR TO THE BOTTOM TO MAKE A DOUBLE CRUST. MOST ANY FRUIT WILL WORK.

Stand by your Pan
Be a Dutch Oven Fan.

74

LOVE ME CHOCOLATE BAR

1 1/2 c flour	1 can Condensed milk
2/3 c sugar	2 eggs
1/4 c brown sugar	1/2 c butter
1 tsp. baking powder	
1/4 tsp. Salt	

1 pkg. peanut butter chips. Mix all dry ingredients together. Set aside. Cut butter into dry ingredients. Beat 2 eggs well and add to dry ingredients. This will make a soft pastry dough. Grease a 12" Dutch Oven and cover bottom of oven with dough. Put flour mixture in crust. Pour over 1 can of condensed milk, add peanut butter chips and sprinkle coconut over top if you want. Makes a great chocolate bar.

NORTH WEST CHOCOLATE CAKE

BOIL: 2 squares margarine, 1 c water & 3-tbsp. cocoa. POUR IN: 2 c flour, 2 c sugar & 1/2 tsp. salt. ADD: 2 eggs, 1/2 c milk, 1/2 tsp. soda, & 1 tsp. vanilla. Mix and pour into greased and floured Dutch Oven . Using 2/3 rule, Bake at 375 for 35 minutes. Cool and frost with chocolate frosting. This is a very chocolate cake. An excellent dish served with whipped cream or Ice Cream.

- "This is Just as good on the East Coast"

GOD MADE THE WORLD ROUND SO WE COULD NOT SEE TO FAR DOWN THE ROAD.

- "Go FOR this one"

75

PINEAPPLE UPSIDE DOWN BRADBURYS WAY

1/2 c butter
3/4 c brown sugar
8 or 10 slices pineapple
1 yellow cake mix
1 1/2 c pineapple juice, if needed, add water or 7-UP to make full amount
1 tsp. vanilla

Melt butter in 12" Dutch Oven. Add the brown sugar and spread over the bottom. Arrange the pineapple slices around the bottom. Put maraschino cherry in middle of slice if you want to. Put cake mix in a bowl and add the juice. Mix well. Pour slowly over pineapple. Bake 25 to 30 minutes or until top is done and springs back at your touch. Bake at 350 degrees.

THERE IS NO LIMIT TO WHAT YOU CAN ACCOMPLISH IF YOU DON'T CARE WHO GETS THE CREDIT.

Sometimes the friends we make are irreplaceable, I feel that way about a lot of my Scout Friends, The Bradbury family, from Sandy are among those. I was part of their boy's lives through Eagle Scouting and later they call and wave when they see me. This is one of their favorite recipes they shared with me from this book. Be sure to say HI if you see them.

"Thanks Alan & Family"

76

DUDE RANCH BROWNIES ------- A LITTLE ON THE GOURMET SIDE

2 c flour
1/2 c butter or margarine
1 c coffee or water
1/2 c buttermilk
1 tsp. baking soda

2 c sugar
1/2 c shortening
1/4 c dark cocoa
2 eggs
1 tsp. vanilla

Better make a Double Batch These go fast — gone

In a lg. bowl, combine the flour & sugar. In a heavy saucepan, combine butter, shortening, coffee & cocoa. Stir & heat to boiling. Pour boiling mixture over the flour. Add the buttermilk, eggs, baking soda & vanilla. Mix well & pour into a well greased, with butter, DUTCH OVEN. Bake at 350 degrees (page 9 temp. guide) for about 20 minutes. 10 or 11 briquettes in Volcano – 10 bottom 15 top briquettes only

While recipe cooks, prepare your frosting. Melt 1/2 c butter and add 2-tbsp. cocoa & 1/4 c milk. Bring to a boil, mix in powdered sugar & vanilla until frosting is smooth. Pour over brownies as soon as you turn them out of the Dutch Oven on a the lid. Serves about 16 pieces.

TIPS: If you don't have buttermilk, add 2-tsp. vinegar or lemon juice to milk. Let sit 3 minutes it will sour.

Hope your Enjoying the recipe's to here

77

LOG CABIN GRUB FRESH PEACH COBBLER---
" LOVE THAT COOK "

FILLING:
1 c sugar
2 eggs
2 tbsp. cornstarch
1 tsp. nutmeg
4 c peaches (fruit)

COBBLER CRUST:
4 tbsp. sugar
3 tbsp. butter
1-1/2 tsp. baking powder
1/2 tsp. salt   2/3 c milk
1 c flour

In a large bowl mix all the filling ingredients except peaches. Set aside and mix all cobbler ingredients together except milk & butter. Now mix in milk & butter, cutting them into the crust mixture until ball forms. Set aside. Now mix peaches(fruit) into filling mixture & spread into the bottom of a 12 or 14 inch DUTCH OVEN. Crumble or spoon the crust mixture over the filling. Sprinkle cinnamon & sugar over the top. Bake at 350 degrees for 25 to 30 minutes. Serve warm for the best results. 10 to 11 briquettes in Volcano, 10 bottom 15 top briquettes only.

VARIATION: Try putting 1 c of brown sugar on the bottom of the pan to create a double crust.

A TBSP. OF LEMON JUICE SPRINKLED OVER THE FRESH FRUIT & TOSSED, WILL KEEP IT FROM TURNING BROWN AFTER PEELING.

" Good - Good & Great "

78

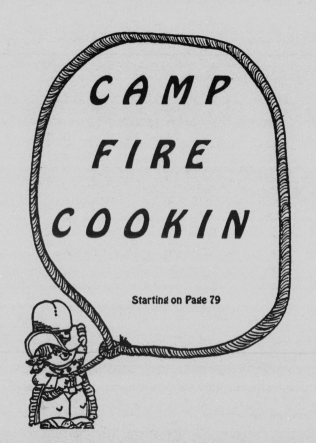

CAMP FIRE COOKIN

Starting on Page 79

&

MISCELLANEOUS

Basic Recipes
for Simple
Cookin

Dessert

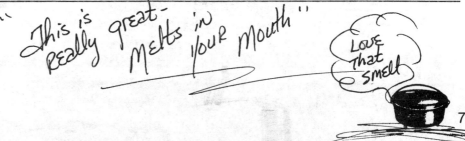

PIONEER HONEY CANDY

When the earlier settlers first came to what is now known as the west, they named it DESERET, which means Honey Bee. The word comes from early Egyptian civilization and rulers wore Honey Bees on their crowns. Because the characteristics of the bee are work and industry, the early pioneers adopted this symbol as there's. They built hives and gathered honey. One of their pleasures was to boil honey until it thickened, and then stretch it as a taffy. Below is the recipe for that taffy.

Mix together 2 cups Honey, 1 cup sugar and 1 cup cream.
Cook over medium heat until it reaches the hard crack stage when dropped in cold water. Pour onto a buttered platter. When cooled enough to handle take small amounts and pull between your hands until it is golden in color and holds a consistent shape. Stretch out long and cut into 1/2 inch pieces. This is great for the kids.

<u>YOU CAN GET ALOT MORE JUICE OUT OF A LEMON IF YOU BOIL IT FOR 3 OR 4 MINUTES BEFORE USING.</u>

"This is Really great - Melts in your mouth"

Love that smell

79

TERIYAKI SAUCE ALA GREAT

Good on all meats

1-12 oz bottle teriyaki sauce
1-4 oz bottle hickory smoked bar-b-Que. sauce
1 tbsp. liquid smoke
1 tsp. Worcestershire sauce

Blend all ingredients together. Pour over meat and let stand for 1 hour. Use some of this mixture with which to cook your meat. The flavor increases the longer it cooks, so check it often. Save remaining juice to use again later. Refrigerate.

POTATOES SOAKED IN SALT WATER FOR 20 MINUTES PRIOR TO BAKING, WILL BAKE MORE RAPIDLY.

YOU CAN'T STOP BUTTER TOFFEE DELUXE

1 Cup butter---1 CUP BROWN SUGAR: Bring butter & sugar to a boil, on low heat, boil for 10 minutes, stirring constantly. Pour in 9x13 greased pan and top with chocolate chips and nuts if desired. Cool and cut.

YOU CAN TURN YOUR DUTCH OVEN LID UPSIDE DOWN ON ROCKS WITH BRIQUETS UNDER IT AND USE IT AS A GRILL.

80

CORN DOG TWISTS BY DOGGY

2 pkg.'s of corn bread twists (grocery store refrigeration)
16 hot dogs
16 Popsicle sticks
melted margarine
Parmesan cheese

"These are great to do with Kids"

Insert stick in bottom of dog. (which end is bottom?) Wrap corn twist around the dog. Cook over campfire and brush with margarine. Sprinkle on Parmesan cheese and devour. (that's eat in English).

SCOUT (cold day) WARMER UPPER

1 gallon apple cider
1 c brown sugar

3 cinnamon sticks
10 whole cloves

Heat all ingredients together in a large pan over a flame. Be careful not to boil as the cinnamon and cloves will break apart and the drink will become lumpy. After 3 or 4 minutes of heat, remove the cinnamon sticks and cloves. Serve warm and its great used inside on cold mornings too.

CHICKEN FRIED CRICKETS
(COURTESY TROOP 411)

It is a little known fact that John C. Fremont was a cricket connoisseur and was originally drawn to the west by the annual cricket festival held by the Indians each spring. Even in his wildest dreams he had not imagined the millions of crickets that awaited his palate and he soon grew tired of the taste. Borrowing a trick from the pioneers of the era, he breaded the crickets and pan-fried them. The recipe below is true to the original "one herb & spice", "finger lickn' good" taste treat.

**1 qt. fresh crickets *	2 tbsp. minced wild onion.
2 tbsp. sage	1 egg
1 c flour	water as needed

This one will bring smiles

Combine batter ingredients with enough water to make a thick batter. Add crickets to the batter and soak for 30 minutes. Pan fry over medium heat until lightly browned. Serve immediately or they loose their flavor.
 * *preferably still kicking*
**(BEEF JERKY CAN BE SUBSTITUTED FOR CRICKETS IF NOT AVAILABLE).

Nothing more fun than cook'n with kids —

SCOUT STYLE DUTCH OVEN CHICKEN

Put enough cooking oil in a hot oven to cover the botto. Roll chicken pieces in flour and put in the oven with the oil. Season with salt, pepper, season salt, garlic salt, onion salt and a touch of cumin or 1 tbsp. Log Cabin Seasoning. Cover and cook. About 30 to 35 minutes. DUTCH OVEN size will depend on how many people you are serving. Try to maintain a 350 degree temperature over an open fire or follow the temperature guide on page 9. Oven can be filled ¾ full if necessary..

Variations: Fill Dutch Oven ½ full of chicken and add carrots, onions and potatoes to fill. Sprinkle with seasoning or salt & pepper

Get the kids involved they will Love it.

STEWY SCOUT DUMPLINGS

(FOR 8)
2 lbs. Hamburger   1 med. Chopped Onion
6 or 8 thin sliced carrots
2 tomatoes sliced
2 cans kernel corn drained
3 cups Bbisquick
1 cup milk

"Habit forming"

Grease 12" DUTCH OVEN and place all ingredients in except the Bisquick and milk. Season with salt, pepper & onion salt. Cover and cook for 25 minutes at 350 degrees. Remove from heat, mix milk & Bisquick and drop by spoons full into stew mixture. Cook another 15 min. covered. Great taste.

These little dinners can be cooked for individuals in small clean tin cans.

83

CORN ON THE COB COOKIN

Pull back the husks on the corn, but do not remove from ear. Remove the silks and soak in water for 20 minutes. Drain well. Spread ears with margarine and salt and pepper. Sprinkle each ear with Parmesan cheese or crushed basil leaves or Italian dressing. Replace husks and grill over the campfire for 30 minutes, Turning frequently until tender. You can also roast in the hot coals for 20 minutes wrapped in foil and turn only once. Its a great outdoor cooking idea for kids.

CAMP TRIPS ARE GREAT IF YOU KEEP THE KIDS BUSY.

" Use your imagination "

CHILI BEAN CHEESE DIP

In a 10" Dutch Oven cook 1 lb. Hamburger, ½ lb. Sausage 1 large onion.
Add 1 lg. Can of beans, 1 lg. Can chili, 1/3 cup BBQ sauce, 1 Cup chopped Red peppers. Warm then add 2 cups cheese. Stir and serve on chips or crackers

Great on Baked Potatoes or buns

This is really Great - To good to be TRUE

84

POPCORN DONE CARAMEL DUTCH

In a 12 or 14" DUTCH OVEN put 1 cup white Karo syrup and 1 c brown sugar. Bring to a boil & add 1/4 cup butter or margarine & 1 small can condensed milk. Stir until butter melts. slow boil for 2 to 3 min. Pour in 6 or 8 cups already popped corn. Stir until the corn is coated and pour out on foil. Let the kids break and eat when slightly cooled. The syrup will be very hot so be careful not to get burned. This is a great treat for campfire time. While oven is warm, spray with Vinegar water mixture and wipe warm DUTCH OVEN. Allow to dry over heat, cool and put in paper towel to store.

YELLOW ZONKERS POPCORN

2 cubes margarine or butter
1-1/3 c sugar 1 tsp. Vanilla
1/2 c Karo syrup

"a kids favorite"

Bring ingredients to a full boil, stirring constantly. Remove most of the heat and let the syrup slow boil for 10 minutes. Add 1-tsp. vanilla and pour over popped corn. About 14 to 16 cups. Turn out on foil & let cool to prevent burns. These campfire ideas can make your hike or camp trip a lot more interesting. Besides its another way to use your DUTCH OVEN.

OVENS ARE EASY TO CLEAN IF YOU DO IT WHILE THEY'RE WARM.

"Heat em up to dry em Out"

85

PEANUT BUTTER CAMP PUPS

Split a hot dog down the middle, and be careful not to split all the way through. Spread the cut surfaces with peanut butter, wrap a slice of bacon around the outside and secure it with a toothpick. Cook over the coals of the fire, turning until the bacon is crisp. This can be served with chips or potato salad, which most kids love. You probably won't be able to talk many grown ups into eating these, but they are pretty good and very different from what you would expect.

SCOUT FRUIT COBBLER

In order for this recipe to turn out it must be followed to the exact measurements.

Precise detail is important.
Put a large can of cherry pie filling into a 10" Dutch Oven. Dump a cherry chip cake mix over the top. Open a can of cherry 7-up and take 2 swallows. Ad some to the cake mix & take 2 more swallows. Add the rest and cover and bake for 25 minutes at 350 degrees.

HELPFUL HINTS FOR TRUE DUTCH OVEN COBBLERS:
Make sure the ingredients used are the ones on sale. If you don't buy an inexpensive brand it may not turn out. When you open the 7-up, be sure to drink some, pour some in and drink some more. Pour the rest in and this will make the cook happy so the cobbler will turn out.

" You got it
This one was created
By kids "

TRADITIONAL CAMP GADGETS
(THIS WILL MAKE IT EASIER.)

When ever we go camping, whether in a metal tent or in a canvas tent, I like to build things and keep my grandkids busy. It's also exciting to see if I can retain my scout survival training. I would just as soon wash-up and cook outside if it's not to cold.

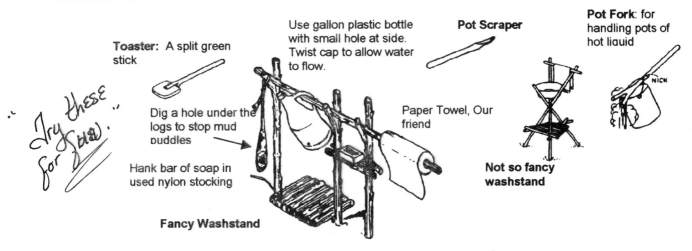

Toaster: A split green stick

Dig a hole under the logs to stop mud puddles

Hank bar of soap in used nylon stocking

Fancy Washstand

Use gallon plastic bottle with small hole at side. Twist cap to allow water to flow.

Paper Towel, Our friend

Pot Scraper

Pot Fork: for handling pots of hot liquid

Not so fancy washstand

Try these for

87

MORE CAMPSITE HELPERS CONT.

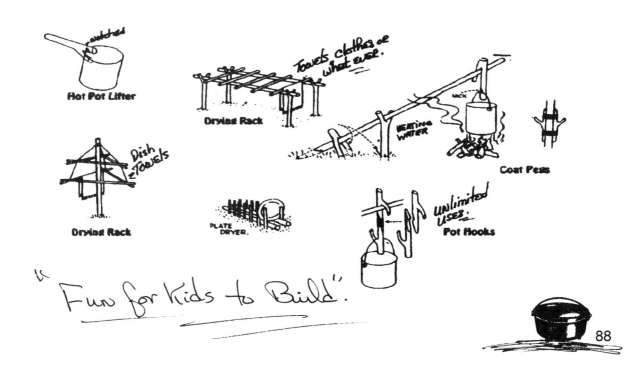

notched

Hot Pot Lifter

Drying Rack

Towels, clothes or what else.

HEATING WATER

WICK

Coat Pegs

Dish Towels

Drying Rack

PLATE DRYER.

unlimited uses.

Pot Hooks

" Fun for Kids to Build".

MORE HANDY CAMP GADGETS CONT.

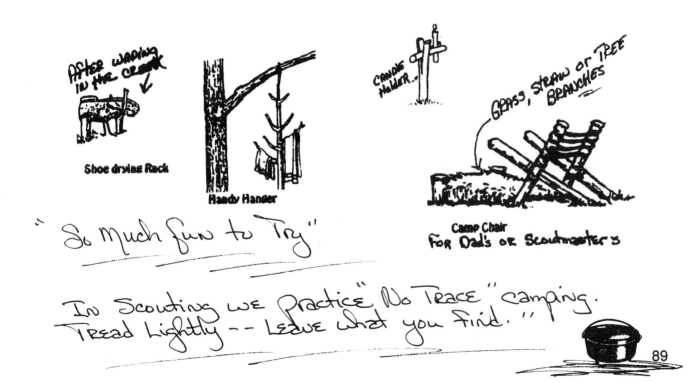

After wading in the creek

Shoe drying Rack

Handy Hanger

Canoe Holder

Grass, Straw or Tree Branches

Camp Chair
For Dad's or Scoutmaster's

" So Much fun to Try "

In Scouting we practice "No Trace" camping.
Tread Lightly -- Leave what you find. "

HELPFUL HINTS TO COOK OVER THE COALS

COOKING FISH can be quite easy: Clean your fish, fillet if you want, Place on a piece of foil that is big enough to completely wrap around the fish. Grease the paper and salt and pepper the fish. Dot with butter if you want. Wrap with foil. Now wrap with 5 or 6 sheets of newspaper and tie with cord. Dip in a bowl to completely soak with water. Carefully squeeze out excess water and place on hot coals. Fish should be cooked by the time the paper begins to char. Fish can be brushed with barbecue sauce, lemon pepper, butter and garlic and cooked in a Dutch Oven 15 minutes.

" It's hard to eat just 1 piece. "

GARLIC BREAD; To feed 5 people, you will need a standard loaf of French Bread. Cut the bread 3/4 of the way through, not separating the bottoms. Mix butter and Garlic Powder together, spread on each side of the bread slices and wrap loosely with 2 pieces of foil to completely cover. Now place on hot coals for 15 minutes. Turn several times. Parmesan Cheese can be mixed with the butter mixture for more flavor.

BURGERS IN LEAVES; You can put 3 leaves of cabbage directly on the coals and place a burger patty on top. Salt & pepper, leave 8 to 10 minutes and turn over onto 3 new leaves. Repeat till meat is cooked through. OR--- you can wrap in foil, cook and eat the cooked cabbage too.

" Let your Dutch Oven do the talking "

90

COWBOY BUNS
THIS WILL FEED 8 PEOPLE

1 cup Baking mix-bisquick
(found on page 41 Log Cabin cookbook)

1/4 c brown sugar	2 eggs
1/4 c melted butter	1 apple

1/4 tsp. cinnamon & nutmeg
1 c milk

Mix all dry ingredients together, add the beaten eggs, milk & butter. Mix to smooth batter. Put cupcake papers in 12" DUTCH OVEN or make foil cups. Divide mixture in cups. Cut apple into slivers and make a design on top of dough. Sprinkle with sugar and cinnamon. Bake covered for 20-min. check if done, bake longer if necessary. 375 degrees.

TIP: If baking over coals, for campfire cookin, be sure to watch closely and not get hot enough to burn. Turn foil over often.

BAKING MIX

9 cups flour, 4 tsp. salt, 1/3 c baking powder, 2 tsp., sugar, 1-1/4 c powdered milk, 1-1/2 c shortening. ¾ Cup powdered eggs

(Great for Lots of Reason's)

Mix all dry ingredients. & cut shortening into mixture until coarse like corn meal. Store in cool covered glass jar. Makes 13 cups. Use as bisquick, add eggs and water to mix. Stores along time. Can be placed in zip lock bags 2 cups each. Use as you need it for biscuits, hot cakes, dumplings crust etc.

" Use these to please others "

91

BAR-B-QUE SAUCE ALA QUICK

1-15 oz can tomato sauce
1/2 c brown sugar
1 tbsp. vinegar
1/2 tsp. mustard
1/2 finely chopped onion
1 tsp. liquid smoke
1 tsp. salt
1/2 tsp. pepper

Mix ingredients together and if you wish, crumble up 4 strips crisp bacon and add to mixture. Green pepper, celery, green onions, or 1 tsp. of Worcestershire sauce add a nice variety. This is great over any kind of meat or to make sloppy Joe's for a large group.

Put 1/2 C. Grated Carrots in for a little sweeter taste.

HOT FUDGE SAUCE

2 sticks butter (1 cup)
3 c sugar
1 can evaporated milk
1/2 tsp. Salt
1/2 c. cocoa or 4 squares of chocolate

Melt butter & chocolate in a double boiler, or in a Dutch Oven over a very low heat. Stir in sugar a little at a time. Dissolve well. Mix will become thick & dry. Stir in very slowly, the evaporated milk. Becomes an excellent chocolate sauce for many uses
Hot chocolate over Ice Cream, Cake or pie

Get ready mouth – here it comes.

92

COWBOY DINNER SCOUT STYLE (TODAYS SCOUTS OR TRAIL SCOUTS)

1 medium potato
1/4 c green beans
4 slices of bacon
1/4 c onion chopped
1/2 c chopped leftover beef or hamburger patty

On a piece of foil about 10 inches square, lay two pieces of bacon 1 inch apart. Place green beans on bacon & put onion on top of beans. Next slice the washed potato with skin on, and place a layer on the onions. Then beef, more onion and remainder of potato. Salt and pepper, fold any bacon up on food pile and fold up the ends of foil. Wrap with a second piece of foil & Place on hot coals. Bake for 15 minutes each side. Turn often if coals are real hot.

TO MAKE A DUTCH OVEN MEAL, JUST 4 TIMES THE RECIPE, GREASE YOUR 10"OVEN AND BAKE AT 350 FOR 25 MINUTES OR WAIT FOR THE SMELL.

"Thats Ms. Dutch Oven to you"

"I Keep Em Hot."

93

CAMPFIRE VEGETABLES

To serve 6 people you will need:
6 potatoes quartered
6 medium onions quartered
24 mushrooms
1 red pepper
1 green onion
12 small tomatoes
1/2 c butter melted
salt, pepper & garlic salt

(Brush often with melted butter)

Let the kids cook these

They will love 'em"

On six roasting sticks, alternate the vegetables except for the tomatoes. Put the seasoning in the melted butter and brush onto the vegetables. Cook the veggies over the hot coals for 5 minutes continuously turning the kabob. After the 5 minutes, add the tomatoes to the end and continue cooking for another 5 minutes. If you use an open campfire, be sure not to let the flames lick at the vegetables as they will shrivel up and dry them out. It is better to use the coals. If you wish to use meat, be sure to cook it first or use left-over roast, steak or chops. This is a great way to use up leftover pork chops or stew meat.

wait for the smell

94

PIT ROASTING FOR TURKEYS AND HAMS

"This is the Pits!"

The first thing to do is dig your pit as deep as necessary to roast what ever it is you have to roast. If you have a 12 lb. ham and a 12 lb. turkey, you will need to dig a pit approximately 36 by 36. Inches that is. Build your fire in the pit, so you can start to build up the coals you need to roast. After building a real good coal base, be sure to part the coals to each end in order to prepare the bed for your meats. If need be, throw in some briquettes to help build the base about 10 minutes before putting in the meat. Prepare the meat, by rubbing the down with bacon grease or oil. If you wish to salt and pepper, now is the time. If you are stuffing your turkey, be sure to do so before you begin preparation to bury it. Wrap each piece of meat individually in heavy foil 3 or 4 times. Wrapping slivered pieces of fresh cut apples, will help to keep the meat moist. The walls of the pit should be real warm after about 1 hour of burning. Spread the coals out in the pit and lay the meats Wrapped in several wet gunnysacks in the middle of the coals. Cover with more wet Gunnysacks or lots of wet newspapers. Cover the meats with the soil you dug out of the whole. Time your baking to about 1 hr. per 3lbs meat. If your meats are close in weight, it helps to judge your timing. When time is up, uncover, unwrap and enjoy. Sometimes an extra 1/2 hour helps to assure you the meat is done.

SPRAY YOUR MEATS WITH THE VINEGAR WATER MIXTURE TO ASSURE GOOD CLEAN MEATS AND TENDERNESS

It's a fun way to try.

← Dirt

← Hot Coals

95

PIONEER SURVIVAL JELLY

WHEN THE PIONEERS CAME ACROSS OUR COUNTRY HEADING WEST, IT GOT REAL TOUGH AT TIMES. WHEN WINTER CAME EARLY, THEY SOMETIMES HAD TO DO WHAT EVER THEY COULD TO STAY ALIVE. WHEN THE MORMON PIONEERS CAME ACROSS, SOME OF THEM GOT CAUGHT IN WYOMING IN AN EARLY STORM NEAR INDEPENDENCE ROCK. TO STAY ALIVE WAS A REAL CHALLENGE. THEY LEFT THEIR POSSESSIONS WITH 4 MEN AND WENT ON WITH ONLY WHAT THEY HAD ON THEIR BACK. THE MEN SURVIVED WITH WHAT THE COULD TO LIVE THRU THE WINTER. BELOW IS AN ACTUAL RECIPE THEY USED TO STAY ALIVE. SEE IF YOU THINK YOU COULD LIVE ON THIS FOR 2 MONTHS.??.

HIDE OF ONE STARVED COW. SCORCH AND SCRAPE OFF THE HAIR. BOIL ONE HOUR IN PLENTY OF WATER, THEN THROW AWAY THE WATER (THIS WILL EXTRACT THE GLUE). WASH AND SCRAPE AGAIN THOROUGHLY. BOIL TO A JELLY AND LET COOL. SPRINKLE WITH SUGAR IF YOU HAVE ANY. BLESS YOUR STOMACHS TO ADJUST TO THE EATING OF THIS FOOD. THEY WILL NEED IT. THIS IS AN ACTUAL TRUE RECIPE THAT THE MARTIN HANDCART COMPANY USED, CAUSE I HAD A RELATIVE IN THAT COMPANY AND HAVE IT RECORDED IN MY HISTORIES.

<u>USING A DUTCH OVEN OUTDOORS DURING HOT WEATHER WILL CUT DOWN ON THE HEAT IN THE HOUSE.</u>

" A True story - a bit of History "

96

THE FOLLOWIG RECIPES ARE SOME OF MY FAVORITES

PORK SAUSAGE & EGG CASSEROLE

1 lb. bulk country sausage
6 hard boiled eggs
1/4 c butter or margarine melted
1/4 tsp. pepper
1 can corn

1/4 c flour
1/2 tsp. onion salt
1/2 tsp. salt
2 c milk
1-1/2 c soft bread crumbs

" A Breakfast "
Favorite
" Um-Um-Good '

Cook sausage in heavy fry pan and drain off the grease. Set aside. In a greased DUTCH OVEN, slice 1/2 of the boiled eggs and arrange on bottom of pot. Melt the butter in a small saucepan and add the flour, salt and pepper. Add milk all at once and stir until mixture thickens as a white sauce. Pour sausage over the eggs, add drained corn and pour white sauce over the top. Slice remaining eggs and arrange over the top of sausage mixture. Sprinkle the bread crumbs over the top and bake for 20 minutes at 350 degrees. A 12" DUTCH OVEN will work nicely for this recipe. This is a great breakfast dish. You can serve this in tortillas with a small amount of salsa for a great variety.

Remember, creativity is very important in **DUTCH OVEN** cooking.

Don't be afraid to try something
new.

97

PORK CHOPS AND RICE

Deliciously Different

10 thinly sliced pork chops
1 lb. of rice (2 cups)
2 cans onion soup
2 cans cream mushroom soup
1 can sliced mushrooms

Brown pork chops in DUTCH OVEN, remove and set aside. Mix rice, soups mushrooms & 3 soup cans of water in DUTCH OVEN. Lay browned pork chops on top of rice mixture. Bake in oven 45 minutes at 350 degrees. Mixture will thicken, rice will cook and pork chops will be very tender.

VARIATION: Substitute chicken or round steak.

PORK GONE DUTCH TERIYAKI

4 to 6 cups pork stew meat
teriyaki sauce Recipe on page 80
1 medium sliced onion
1 can mushrooms drained

Put pork in greased 12" Dutch oven and brown on both sides. Add all other ingredients and cook for 1 hour at 325 to 350 degrees. Can be served over rice or mashed potatoes on noodles or with stir fry vegetables. It's a great surprise to most people.

VARIATION: try chicken instead of pork.

REMEMBER TO DRY YOUR CAST IRON BY HEATING IT UP AFTER WASHING. MAKE SOME MEMORIES WITH A DUTCH OVEN AND THROUGH A BLOCK PARTY.

The Smell

SCOUT BREAKFAST CASSEROLE

2 apples, peeled & sliced
2 lbs. sausage
9 slices bread, cubed
3/4 tsp. mustard (optional)
9 eggs, beaten
3 c milk
1 c. shredded cheese

Cook and drain sausage, sauté apples in sausage drippings, add all other ingredients & mix together. Bake in 12" Dutch Oven for 35 to 45 minutes. Makes a tasty breakfast casserole. Can be served with syrup. In your Volcano use 10 Briquettes. 10 bottom 15 top briquettes only. 350 in your oven.

"Cooks my Name Dutch Oven's my Game"

TOAD IN HOLE BREAKFAST

1 lb. link sausage
1 cup flour
2 eggs
½ tsp. Salt

Cook sausage in 12" Dutch Oven at a high heat. Brown them well (350 to 400 degrees). Mix all other ingredients together. Take ½ of the drippings from sausage and arrange links around the bottom of the pot. Pour batter on top, cover & bake. Batter will puff up. Cut into squares & serve with jam or syrup 20 to 25 minutes. In your Volcano use only 10 briquettes. Eggs burn fast! No middle bottom heat. 350 in your oven at home. 10 bottom, 15 top briquettes only.

Breakfast To make campin fun.

99

HONEY GLAZED CARROTS

10 carrots peeled and sliced
1/2 c honey
1/4 c butter
2 tbsp. brown sugar

Simply Scrumptous

Put butter in 10" DUTCH OVEN, melt and add carrots. Pour honey over the top and sprinkle with brown sugar. Cover and bake on a low heat, 325 degrees for 30 minutes or until tender. Meanwhile, prepare meat dish.

" Add a Cut up Sweet Potato "

JUST WAIT FOR THE SMELL, YOUR OVEN WILL TELL YOU WHEN IT'S DONE. BE SURE TO HEAT YOUR OVEN AND DRY IT OUT THOROUGHLY BEFORE STORING.

ALL IN ONE POTATO BREAKFAST

1 large pkg. Hashbrowns
2 lbs. Ground sausage
8 eggs scrambled
10 oz. Shredded cheese

In a 12" Dutch Oven, brown the sausage. Remove meat and add hashbrowns in sausage drippings. Smooth out on bottom of oven and spread sausage on top. Spread the cheese over sausage. Beat eggs and add milk and pour over the mixture. Cover and cook with very little heat on bottom. Should take about 14 to 20 minutes

IF YOU HAVE TO SPEED TO GET SOMEWEAR THEN MAYBE YOU SHOULD HAVE LEFT YEATERDAY.

100

Dandelion Soup

2 cups cooked chicken cut up
3 cans cream chicken soup
5 cups water
½ cup minute rice
1 tsp. Real salt and ½ tsp. Black pepper
4 cups young tender dandelion greens cut or torn.

Dried Roots make a coffee (')

Pick Leaves before they blossom young & tender"

Combine soups, chicken, water, salt and pepper in a 12" Dutch Oven. Bring to a slow simmer. Add rice and greens. Cover and simmer for 5 to 6 minutes. Spinach can be used when dandelion is not available. Serve over toast or mashed potatoes if desired. Or boil up enough rice to serve with soup also. This is a great way to show kids how good fresh dandelions can be. Don't be afraid to try this, it really is good. Always pick the leaves before the plant goes to seed and wash off in water.

Gooseberry Pie
– Line your pie plate with puff (pie crust) and fill with fresh gooseberries or gooseberry pie filling. Sprinkle 1 cup sugar over the gooseberries and sprinkle on 2 tbsp. Flour. Put a few chunks of butter around on the top, and cover with a top crust. Some pioneers would bake the crust on top only, calling it a gooseberry cobbler. Bake until golden brown in a 12" Dutch Oven, with 15 briquettes on top and 8 on the bottom or, in you own oven at 350 degrees until crust is brown. Gooseberry pie filling is available in most canned fruit sections of your supermarket now. One of the best pies ever made. Blueberries, blackberries, raspberries and such can be baked the same way. You can use brown sugar instead of white If you want.

101

Danish Aebleskivers
"A Danish Sweet Bread"

Aunt Winnie's specialty

There Gre---at.

"These are a real Special Treat"

2 cups buttermilk or 4 tbsp.
powdered buttermilk and 2 cups water
3 eggs
1 tsp. Baking powder

½ tsp. Real salt   1 tsp. Soda
2 tsp. Sugar
Cinnamon or Nutmeg optional

Warm and lightly oil your aebleskiver pan or put 2 inches of oil in a 10" Dutch oven. Let pan slowly heat up as you mix the bread. Break and separate the eggs, and beat the yolks. Add sugar, salt and milk to the egg yolks. Mix in the flour, soda and baking powder. Mix well. Beat egg whites or if camping fluff them well with a hand beater or fork. Add to the flour mix and place a tbsp. of mix in the egg pan. You can drop by the spoon full in the hot oil and cook one side. Turn over and cook other side. Roll in cinnamon and sugar, powdered sugar or eat with butter and jam. You can add applesauce to the mix, raisins, cheese, cherries or what ever you like. A can of kernel corn drained is also very good.

"History Tip" When the pioneers came across the plains, there was not always time to cook breads, especially when traveling. So Johnny cakes, dumplings, sour dough biscuits and pancakes were used. The common grains used were wheat for strength, rice for extra energy, and corn for heat. Graham flour was named after Sylvester Graham. He was ordained minister who was considered a food reformer and preached about the benefits of wheat flour. Whole wheat flour, (Graham Flour) and Graham crackers were named for him.

102

Sweet Potato Balls

Boil, peel and mash 4 sweet potatoes. Add ¼ cup sweet cream or milk, 3 tbs. Butter, ½ tsp. Lemon juice or peel, 3 tsp. Brown sugar, 1 tsp. Real salt. Shape mixture into balls and dip into beaten eggs then into cracker or breadcrumbs. Fry in pan or Dutch Oven until brown. These can be served as is or you can bake them in your Dutch Oven with meatballs and serve as a min dish. Cream gravy or a can of mushroom soup can be poured over the top to bake also. If you wish to serve them as a dessert, just simply serve with maple syrup.

Deep-fried Potato Balls

Mix 4 cups of left over mashed potatoes and add 2 tsp. Log Cabin or Volcano all purpose seasoning, ½ cup milk or cream, and 3 medium eggs in a pan and slowly warm. Stir and cook for about 2 minutes. This can be done ahead of time. Cool, drop large tbsp. size balls in cracker crumbs or breadcrumbs and roll to cover completely. Can be dipped again in beaten egg mixture and rolled again in crumbs. Drop in hot oil in a 10 or 12" Dutch oven. Fry and serve with Chili sauce, Salsa, Gravies, Cheese Sauce or what ever. Great snack for camping or at home.

Fried Cucumbers

Wash and slice cucumbers, squash, green tomatoes, egg plant, zucchini or what ever and dip in beaten egg mix and roll in cracker or bread crumbs. Fry in hot oil pan. Sprinkle with Real salt, pepper, onion salt and garlic. Turn over and fry till brown. This is a great veggie dish. Try using different crackers and types of breadcrumbs

103

Ross's Specialty beans

1 large can red kidney beans
1 large can pork and beans
1 large can chili and beans
1 large can crushed pineapple
1 red pepper, green pepper
and onion chopped

2 tbsp. barbecue sauce
2 tbsp. Worcestershire sauce
1 lb. Bacon ½ tsp. Black pepper
1 large pkg. Lil smokies sausages

This is Ross Taylor's recipe — Great Guy — owner of Rocky Mtn Volcano

Cook bacon cut into little pieces with red and green peppers and onion. Add sauces and all the beans to the mixture in a 12" Dutch Oven. Drain the pineapple and add to the bean mixture. Flavor with a little teriyaki sauce if so desired and simmer for 10 minutes. Serve with any meat dish or potatoes. Any type of bread will go well with these beans. You can add left over chopped pork or beef or chicken if so desired. Even lamb tastes good with this dish. Do not over cook, as the beans will go mushy if boiled too long. In a 12 inch Dutch Oven the beans will stay warm for 20 to 30 minutes. This dish is also good over corn bread. Double or triple the recipe for larger groups. Easy to use for big dinners with corn on the cob or green vegetables. You can add chili sauce, stewed tomatoes, grits, hominy, potatoes or a variety of things to stretch your beans for bigger groups.

STRANGE THAT WE CALL MONEY DOUGH, DOUGH USUALLY STICKS TO YOUR FINGERS!

I'm ready

ONE POT GREEN BEAN SUPPER

In a 10 or 12" skillet, or a 12" Dutch Oven that has been warmed and lightly greased, fry 2 lbs. of hamburger and one diced medium size onion. When fully cooked, drain off the excess grease and add 4 tbsp. of your favorite steak sauce or Worcestershire sauce. Put in 2 pkgs. Of frozen green style green beans, 2 can cream of celery soup and 2 cans mushroom pieces-drained. Stir enough to mix. Heat to simmering boil, cover for 10 minutes. Sprinkle with garlic croutons or crushed Ritz crackers just before serving.

Wildlife: Respect for others in the outdoors also includes the wildlife. Keeping a safe distance from birds and animals will not force them to flee and you'll be able to enjoy them more. We can greatly effect the wildlife by destroying their habitat, so be very careful not to do so when you are hiking or camping. If you travel with a pet, never allow it to harass the wildlife. One of the neatest things is to observe the wildlife and have them come close enough to almost touch. I have actually had a deer nudge my hand because I was so still. There is nothing as exciting as watching a busy little squirrel or chip monk gather their food for storage and have them run across your lap as you sit quietly and watch. It's your outdoors, lets all protect it for future generations.

Great Words to Read by:

105

Sloppy Joes Simple Style

1 lb. Hamburger
1 onion chopped
¼ cup chopped celery
1 lb. Bacon
2 tbsp. mustard
1 can chicken gumbo soup
½ cup water
4 to 5 tbsp. ketchup

Warm and oil a 12" Dutch Oven. Place first 4 ingredients in the pot and sauté'. Add the remaining ingredients and simmer. Serve on buns or eat with crackers like chili. Easy to make and great to eat.

These are great for Tailgate Parties

Canyon Meatballs and Beans

2 lbs. Hamburger made into balls
2 cans green beans or pinto beans
1 envelope onion soup mix
2 cans cream mushroom soup
2 cups sour cream
½ cup water

Warm and oil a 12" Dutch Oven. Place the meatballs in the oven and put all other ingredients in with them. Cover and bake slowly at 350 degrees for 30 minutes. 12 briquettes in your Volcano. Briquettes only, 10 bottom and 15 top. In the Log Cabin stove, use only 12 briquettes on the bottom. In you oven, place on 350 and wait for the smell. This will have a great taste.

Mississippi Chili --- Texas Style

Preheat and oil a 12" Dutch Oven. Place the following in layers until the oven is bout 1/3 full. Bake on 12 Briquettes only. In your own oven at home, place the Dutch oven on a cookie sheet and bake at 350 and wait for the smell. Should take about 35 to 40 minutes. Enjoy, this one is worth it.

    Hominy
    Chopped Onions
    Chili with no beans
    Grated Cheese

You'll be pleasantly surprised at the unique taste of this chili.

1. Quick Main Dish
2. Warm and oil a 10" Dutch Oven
3. Slice Onions in the bottom
4. Slice potatoes over the onions
5. Crumble hamburger over the potatoes
6. Mix 1 can mushroom, celery, potato, vegetable or other soup and pour over top
7. Season with garlic salt and Real salt and pepper
8. Cook on campfire, briquettes, your oven or camp chef for 1 hour
9. Do not get fire so hot to boil meal

Sprinkle with cheese, bacon bits, finely chopped peppers or celery or what ever sounds good.

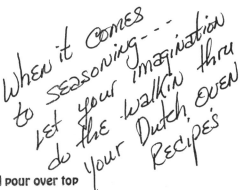

When it comes to seasoning--- Let your imagination do the walkin thru your Dutch Oven Recipes

107

Great time saving ideas

Save all gravies, they have great leftover uses
Grease inner rim of pans to prevent most boil overs
Soaking used pots with water immediately after use makes them easier to clean
Newspaper and paper bags are handy to peal vegetables on.
Keeping kitchen knives sharp is important to a good cook
Lemon Juice will remove stains and odors from hands and cutting boards.
A small wooden cutting board will save on countertop and clean up in dishwater.
Salt and lemon juice will remove burns from enamel pans
Cover all foods when placing in refrigerator.
An open container of baking soda placed in refrigerator will absorb odors. Exchange ever 2 to 3 months for freshness.
Adding curry powder to creamed vegetables is like having a safety pin when a zipper breaks.

ADD SOME OF THESE TO YOUR CHILI, CRUMBLES BACON, CRACKERS, CHEESE, SOUR CREAM, ONIONS, KETCHUP, PEPPER, MUSTARD

"we got a million of them"

"Nothin says Lovin — Like cookin in a Dutch Oven."

108

SOME HELPFUL HINTS FOR DUTCH OVEN COOKING

When you are cooking yeast breads or rolls in your DUTCH OVEN, put it inside and put 3 or 4 briquettes on top. It will help the dough to rise faster and keep it draft free. This provides just the right amount of heat.

Remember to use the 2/3 rule when your are baking in your oven. This will apply to almost every dish so be sure to check your food after 2/3 of the time is up. The more you cook the easier it will get. You'll find that judging the temperature will change in windy conditions and cold weather. Use the chart on page 9 as a guideline but expect to have to adjust it at times. If you are using a Volcano, 10 briquettes on bottom and omit the top heat, just turn the rolls upside down when done, they will be golden brown.

When cleaning your DUTCH OVEN, be sure to scrape out all the charred and stuck food that you can, then spray with Vinegar, return to heat with lid on and it should wipe clean real fast. Clean ovens while hot for easier and faster cleaning. Most of the time you will be able to wipe the oven out while it is still warm. Paper towels will be your best friends.

Re-season your oven anytime you think it needs it. Wipe it out with a clean dry paper towel after each greasing so that it does not have puddles of grease. It will go rancid if you just let it sit.

Use your imagination when cooking. If you want to experiment, let your conscience be your guide. Try a little more sugar or a different spice. Your gonna love this type of cookin and all the compliments. Let me know if I can help or encourage you, I'd like to hear from you with any suggestions or hints that you have to share.

It's the smell that counts

109

MY FAVORITE POEM FROM YESTER-YEAR

Nancy from Snowbird loves this one

FLOUR SACK UNDER WEAR;

When I was a Maiden fair----Mama made our underwear----With five li'l ones & Pa's poor pay-----We can't afford no lingerie----.There were no names or fancy stitches ----not anywhere on our flour sack britches.----there was no lace no fancy pleats-----Just gold medal's seal upon our seats------Those little pant had best of all----a little scene I still recall----Harvesters working, gleaning wheat,-----straight across the little seat.----Tougher than a grizzly bear----Was our flour sack underwear.----Through the years each Jill and Jack,----Wore part of this old white sack.----Waste not want not we soon learned------A penny saved a penny earned.----Tea towels, Curtains , Bedspreads too,----Oh & tablecloths were all reused.----But the best beyond compare,----was our flour sack underwear.

"My Dad used to recite these by heart"

ME MUDDER;

When all me early prayers were said---Who tucked me in me widdle bed---and spanked me bum till it was red---ME MUDDER.---Who lift me from me cozy cot---And placed me on the cold cold pot----and made me wee-wee whether I had to or not,-----ME MUDDER.---And when the morning light had come---And in me crib I'd piddled some---Who wiped me wed-checked wide bum,---ME MUDDER.---Who did my hair so neatly part----And press me gently to her heart,---And sometimes squeeze me till I'd fart,---ME MUDDER.

LOVE DOESN'T MAKE THE WORLD GO ROUND,--LOVE IS WHAT MAKES THE RIDE WORTH WHILE.

110

9-Mile Heritage Expeditions

Linking the Past to the Future
By
Teaching Traditional Back Country Skills

Come join us at 9-mile for a day or a week of great fun.   You may want to participate in Horsemanship and packing classes,   Horse Handling and training,   Cross-cut saw maintenance,   Cross-cut saw certification, Use and care of traditional tools,   Basic Horsemanship,   Defensive horsemanship,   Leave no trace stock course,   Ninemile packing clinics, Advanced horsemanship,   Advanced packing classes or the Traditional Low Impact back country cooking done with Dutch Ovens.   You can learn a lot, eat a lot of good cooking, meet some of the world's best people, make new friends, hear great campfire music and do it all in the beautiful Montana mountains. (-Mile is located about 20 miles west of Missoula, and 4 miles off the main highway. You can wake up to the mules morning serenade, have elk and deer in you front yard, stimulating crisp country morning air and enjoy some of the best conversation you'll ever here.

        I am privileged to be the one who teaches the Dutch oven classes and help feed the crew most of the classes. It's my home away from home and I love it. Ken, Bob, Lynn and almost anyone at 9-Mile will do their best to make you feel welcome. If you go away hungry it's my fault. If you want more info., just call the Ranger station and they will send you a brochure. Or write to **Heritage Expeditions---20325 Remount Rd.—Huson, Mt. 59846**
    Phone 406-626-5201.

111

While Thumbing through this book I found a few favorites

Page #	Name of Recipe	Additions or Changes
1.		
2.		
3.		
4.		
5.		
6.		
7.		
8.		
9.		
10.		

I HOPE YOU HAVE THOROUGHLY ENJOYED YOUR JOURNY THROUGH THIS LITTLE BOOK.
BE SURE TO ADD A LITTLE LOVE TO EACH RECIPE